As parents, we sometimes get stuck in survi⋯ ⋯⋯res of
bad behavior. Dr. Kathy Koch focuses on fii⋯ ⋯⋯;odly
character in our kids by instilling critical core⋯ ⋯⋯t her
insights on raising courageous, compassiona⋯ ⋯⋯ist!

JIM DALY
President, Focus on the Family

As a parent, I have always strived to raise my children with strong character and values, knowing these qualities will shape their lives and impact the world around them. That's why I love this book! In *Parent Differently*, Dr. Kathy Koch explores the fundamental questions of what character truly is and how it can be nurtured in our children. From understanding how children develop mature character to the connection between character and obedience, Dr. Kathy provides a solid foundation for parents to build upon. I felt encouraged and inspired to take an active role in shaping my children's character while acknowledging the unique gifts and strengths they possess. I wholeheartedly recommend this book to parents committed to making a positive difference in their children's lives and the world they inherit!

TRICIA GOYER
Wife, mom, podcast host, and bestselling author of over 80 books, including *Calming Angry Kids: Hope and Help for Parents in the Trenches*

In *Parent Differently*, Dr. Koch draws us back to the core essentials and necessity of biblical character development in our children. In her usual Scripture-based practical gentle leading, she challenges without shaming, inspires without being "preachy," and gives hope without illusion. Way to go, Kathy. Once again, you've knocked it out of the park.

MARK HANCOCK
CEO, Trail Life USA

The Bible shows us that Jesus loved, valued, and celebrated children at a time and in a culture that largely ignored them. This radical example of Jesus is just one insight that Kathy Koch draws out in this book to help parents see the exciting opportunity to shape and build the character of their children. Kathy offers encouragement and practical guidance for parents and caring adults who want to parent differently by suggesting they look first to their own beliefs and values, using those as a springboard for loving and teaching children. Whether you're a parent, grandparent, mentor, or teacher, Kathy's book can inspire you to consider the ways that you can nurture and celebrate the kids in your life and help them thrive as they build biblical character!

KAREN PEARSON
President, Kids Hope USA

Once again, Dr. Kathy has provided sound tools for a parent's toolbox with her latest work, *Parent Differently*. Her no-nonsense approach and clear calls to action will help any parent begin the important journey of character development within their child. This intentional approach to an area of human development that has traditionally been more "caught than taught" will result in a generation of kids that could restore civility and decorum into our culture. Character is king despite one's choice of vocation, and parents need to understand its importance. As a thought leader in youth character development for over three decades, I cannot more heartily endorse *Parent Differently*. It should be a staple in your parenting library!

PATTI GARIBAY
Founder and Executive Director, American Heritage Girls, Inc.

Dr. Kathy has done it again! She has put practical, God-glorifying parenting on an accessible shelf for us all. From, "In the beginning, God," to "The grace of the Lord Jesus be with all," God has revealed to us who He is and that He wants us to be like Him. Not only do we desire to be like Him, but we desire it for our children as well. The enduring question is, how do we get there? Dr. Kathy, with faithfulness to God's Word and sensitivity to His Spirit, has mined from His eternal truth a rich definition of biblical character to help us answer this question. In carefully defining biblical character and walking through the practical expression of it, she encourages us to invite God to go public through our life.

WIL AND MEEKE ADDISON
Homeschooling parents of six; cohosts of *Airing the Addisons*, American Family Radio

Parenting isn't for the faint of heart, especially in these troubling times. And while there are numerous resources on Christian parenting, one rarely comes along that challenges and impacts an entire generation of parents. I believe that this book is one of them. Anchored in how to influence and build biblical character in a child's heart, my prayer is that parents would find strength, courage, hope, and joy as they love on and raise their kids to follow after God.

TIM CLINTON
President, American Association of Christian Counselors; cohost, Dr. James Dobson's *Family Talk*; Executive Director, Liberty University Global Center for Mental Health, Addiction, and Recovery

This is a confusing time to parent children—unless, of course, you are parenting them with the unchanging principles that are found in the Bible. Dr. Kathy uses biblical principles to provide clarity on the issue of character as it relates to raising children. Perhaps there has never been a more important time for this message. In a world that has rejected moral absolutes, Dr. Kathy reminds us to parent differently. Her voice exhorts and encourages parents to follow Jesus as they raise their children in these confusing times. If you are looking for a must-read book on parenting, this one should be in your library!

HEIDI ST. JOHN
Author of *Becoming MomStrong*; host of the Heidi St. John podcast; founder of MomStrongInternational.com

PARENT DIFFERENTLY

Raise Kids with
Biblical Character
That Changes Culture

KATHY KOCH, PhD

MOODY PUBLISHERS

CHICAGO

Unless otherwise indicated, Scripture quotations are from the ESV® Bible (The Holy Bible, English Standard Version®), copyright © 2001 by Crossway, a publishing ministry of Good News Publishers. Used by permission. All rights reserved. The ESV text may not be quoted in any publication made available to the public by a Creative Commons license. The ESV may not be translated in whole or in part into any other language.

Scripture quotations marked (NLT) are taken from the *Holy Bible*, New Living Translation, copyright ©1996, 2004, 2015 by Tyndale House Foundation. Used by permission of Tyndale House Publishers, Carol Stream, Illinois 60188. All rights reserved.

Edited by Betsey Newenhuyse
Interior design: Puckett Smartt
Cover design: Erik Peterson
Cover illustration of tree copyright © 2023 by PPrat/iStock (893873454). All rights reserved.

Library of Congress Cataloging-in-Publication Data

Names: Koch, Kathy, author.
Title: Parent differently : raise kids with biblical character that changes
  culture / Kathy Koch.
Description: Chicago : Moody Publishers, 2023. | Includes bibliographical
  references. | Summary: "Most parents misguidedly prioritize behavior.
  Why and how to instill character. We want children to grow in humility,
  gratitude, and respect--for others and themselves. To be brave,
  compassionate, and joyful--to flourish and live into their God-given
  designs. Koch provides an invaluable resource for shepherding children
  in godly character"-- Provided by publisher.
Identifiers: LCCN 2023021652 (print) | LCCN 2023021653 (ebook) | ISBN
  9780802431189 (paperback) | ISBN 9780802473301 (ebook)
Subjects: LCSH: Parenting--Religious aspects--Christianity. |
  Parenting--Biblical teaching--Christianity. | Child rearing--Religious
  aspects--Christianity. | Child rearing--Biblical teaching--Christianity.
  | Character--Religious aspects--Christianity. | Character--Biblical
  teaching--Christianity. | BISAC: RELIGION / Christian Living / Parenting
  | RELIGION / Christian Living / Family & Relationships
Classification: LCC BV4529 .K629 2023 (print) | LCC BV4529 (ebook) | DDC
  248.8/45--dc23/eng/20230606
LC record available at https://lccn.loc.gov/2023021652
LC ebook record available at https://lccn.loc.gov/2023021653

Originally delivered by fleets of horse-drawn wagons, the affordable paperbacks from D. L. Moody's publishing house resourced the church and served everyday people. Now, after more than 125 years of publishing and ministry, Moody Publishers' mission remains the same—even if our delivery systems have changed a bit. For more information on other books (and resources) created from a biblical perspective, go to www.moodypublishers.com or write to:

Moody Publishers
820 N. LaSalle Boulevard
Chicago, IL 60610

1 3 5 7 9 10 8 6 4 2

Printed in the United States of America

I dedicate this book to my friend Debbie Thompson.
She loves me well and was a fabulous assistant who humbly served.
She consistently exhibits biblical character and glorifies God in her
responses to both positive and negative experiences.
She's a wonderful friend and powerful example of how
to live well, and I'm grateful!

CONTENTS

FOREWORD

Today our kids are living in a cultural firestorm, the likes of which most parents could have never imagined. The agenda to deconstruct reality and silence believers from proclaiming truth is raging hotter with each passing day. We watch as the pillars of civil society are fracturing right before our very eyes, and we wonder . . . how are we supposed to raise our kids in the midst of all this?

With a combined nine kids between the two of us, we know exactly what this feels like.

But you might think it odd for us to say, there's never been a better time to raise kids!

Our children could have been born at any moment in history, but God chose this time. And He's designed them (and us) with the very talents and abilities we need to fight the spiritual battle that's raging today—and win.

And it's up to us as parents to train and equip our kids for victory.

The spiritual climate today reminds us of the time of David and Goliath. Inside that story rests a simple point that is especially helpful for us as parents. When David killed Goliath, the first question King Saul asked David was, "Whose son are you, young man?" (1 Sam. 17:58).

Saul saw something in David he hadn't seen in anyone in Israel, not even in himself. He saw courage. He saw strength. He saw a young man who stood unflinching in the face of certain death and boldly proclaimed God as King. Saul could have asked him a thousand different questions in that moment of awe, but he asked one simple question: "Who's your dad?"

Translation: *Who raised you to have a warrior spirit like this?*

Saul's question reveals the importance of our role as parents to raise up a generation of boys and girls who will stand like David and face the "Goliaths" of today. If David's dad could do it in his generation, we can do it in ours. We serve the same God with the same power—and we face the same enemy.

This is why we're thankful Dr. Kathy chose to write this book. We've seen firsthand how the principles she teaches have influenced our family in powerful ways. Her material has given us practical and powerful tools to train our kids to be people of character, strength, and honor. We can't think of anyone better to help us equip our kids for the fight of their lives—the one we know they will all face.

Most people know us as the twin guys who got fired by HGTV back in 2014 because we wouldn't compromise our biblical values. You might remember us in the days that followed as we were featured on more than two hundred interviews—from FOX News and CNN to ABC's *Nightline* and ESPN—talking about the importance of believers in America standing strong for their faith, whatever the cost. We found ourselves in the midst of a cultural firestorm, face-to-face with a "Goliath" in culture—an evil agenda to silence Christians who stand for biblical truth. By God's grace and the empowerment of the Holy Spirit, we stood strong and refused to back down.

Of course, if you read our book *Whatever the Cost*, you would know how cowardly we were in that intense moment of testing. You would know how the temptation to remain silent about the "politically incorrect" aspects of our faith felt overwhelming. But we stood strong nonetheless.

What people don't know, however, is the way our parents raised us to be warriors long before our moment on the cultural battlefield.

Our dad was a pastor in Dallas, Texas, in the mid-nineties. When he first heard about the travesty of abortion he knew he couldn't sit back and preach nice sermons without doing something about the legalized murder of innocent kids. So he moved his church office next to the busiest abortion clinic in Dallas.

Dad used to say, "If your theology doesn't become biography, then your theology is worthless." His involvement in the pro-life movement when it was largely *politically incorrect* showed us the value of living for Christ whatever the cost. By the time we were sixteen years old, he was removed as pastor from our church because of his stand for life.

We listened as the leaders of the denomination told him he had to choose between being a pastor or being a pro-life advocate. They said he could not do (or be) both. We heard Dad tell them that he had no choice and that if it cost him his church to do what was right and act as salt and light, then so be it.

For the next few years, we watched our dad and other pro-lifers get hauled off to jail often. We witnessed police brutality as they violently dragged him across the pavement and stuffed him into the back of their cars. We watched pro-abortion advocates scream at him, spit in his face, and hurl insults as he was carted off. All the while he never said a word. And we watched our faithful mom stand by his side and encourage him to keep up the fight.

So in the spring of 2014, when we got fired by HGTV and cancel culture set its sights on us to ruin our names and reputations, we remembered our faithful parents. They refused to back down when the same evil agenda attacked them. And it was their example that paved the way for us.

Our dad used to say, "Boys, I'm raising you as sheep among wolves." Dad wasn't concerned about raising us as sheep among sheep. He knew that for us to find out who God made us to be we needed to be *in* the fight, not *protected* from it. In time we discovered a supernatural reality of being sheep among wolves—the lion inside of us was far stronger than the wolf threatening us.

The Lion of the Tribe of Judah (Jesus) is inside each of us, and He gives us all the power we need to stand boldly against the Goliaths in our culture. Just as David took down the giant with a sling and a stone, the book you hold in your hand will give you the weapons you need to outfit your children for the fight!

David had character that was forged into him by his parents. And it was this character that stood and faced down the greatest enemy in Israel's history. This book will help you develop that type of character in your kids and give you the tools you need to train them for our current cultural battle.

The time is now. Get ready to fight and win!

DAVID BENHAM AND JASON BENHAM
Nationally acclaimed entrepreneurs, bestselling authors, speakers
BenhamBrothers.com

What Is
CHARACTER, and Why
Does It MATTER?

After different legs of an unusually long ministry trip, my checked bag didn't reach my destination. Twice! This rarely happens to me, so I was both surprised and frustrated.

Early one morning, I joined a line at the ticket counter to check in for the third part of my itinerary and planned to ask if my bag was there. It may have arrived at the airport on a later flight, but no one notified me or brought it to me. That was my hope.

The line was long because only one attendant staffed the desk. I think everyone was a bit anxious. I was concerned, because asking her to look for my bag would take time. No one would be happy about that.

I felt myself fighting against growing impatience and a critical spirit. I shifted my weight from one foot to the other. I looked at my watch more often than necessary. I often glanced at the woman who was working the counter. She seemed efficient, but I'm sure I wasn't always smiling when I glanced her way.

My negative thoughts and self-talk were interrupted by a woman who approached me from outside the line.

"I don't mean to embarrass you, but are you Kathy Koch?"

I was so stunned I stumbled to even answer with a simple, "Yes."

"Oh my goodness! I thought it was you. I've followed you for years and I love your podcast. The episodes about character have been so good. When will the character book be out?"

I had come so close to exhibiting less-than-great character before that moment, and if I had, my testimony would have been tarnished. I'm grateful my beliefs ruled my behavior, and she interrupted before I might have given in to my frustration and behaved badly.

Why was I able to exhibit patience even though I was concerned about how little time I had before my flight would take off? Why did I keep the growing critical spirit within me silent to others? When I got to the counter and asked about my bag, why could I express gratitude that it was there and not complain that no one had contacted me to say it was there?

WHAT CAUSED ME TO BE PATIENT?

Reflecting on my experience, I realized I was patient because glorifying God through my choices is important to me. Scripture has taught me that our understanding of truth and the Holy Spirit's leading can guide us to make wise decisions. When we don't, we don't represent God well. People might question whether we're truly saved. My beliefs about God and His expectations of me are foundational. I want to be known as someone who follows God well.

Also, I realized I was patient because I have compassion for people. I see what may be wrong and desire to help. I couldn't do much for the attendant, but not acting irritated probably did help her. I didn't criticize her to others or to her face because I think the best of people. I knew it wasn't her fault she was alone at the counter. I expressed gratitude because thankfulness is a high priority for me. It's one of the best ways to stay humble and honor others. A foundational belief is that everyone has value and deserves to be treated respectfully.

I hope this example from my life shows you why you must think about the hopes and goals you have for your children. They will motivate you to prioritize teaching good character and which qualities you emphasize. Who do you want your children to be and become? Character matters today and it determines destiny.

Children can learn to have a positive and complete character. More importantly, children can learn to have a *biblical* character.

These children will use the qualities Jesus used and will be motivated by God's ways and will. They will do the right things even if the burden is heavy and no one is watching.

Thanks for trusting me and spending your valuable time with me. Truths here will empower you to have the best character you can have and teach it to your children. Then they can change culture. Let's start with some basics.

WHAT IS CHARACTER, EXACTLY?

As a child, I wrote invitations to parties, thank-you notes for gifts, get-well cards, and notes to encourage people. Hours and hours. These are my memories.

I've always loved people and writing, but that's not why I sent notes when I was young. I loved the sealing wax and the beautiful "K" seal I pressed into the wax to emboss the envelopes. I made my mark—Kathy with a K is writing you.

I remember being more joyful than you might expect when discovering the word "character" refers to tools that "sharpen, cut in furrows, or engrave" to create a "distinctive differentiating mark."[1]

This appeals to me. I want my character to define me. I want the same for you and your children. Character consists of our moral qualities, ethical standards, and principles. It's observable, forms our reputation, determines our priorities, is based on beliefs and values, and, therefore, serves as our inner governance.[2] It is within our control, a benefit to us and everyone we interact with, and something that can improve.

Os Guinness communicates the concept of being marked by our character this way: "Character is the inner form that makes anyone or anything what it is—whether a person, a wine, or a historical period. . . . Applied to a person, it is the essential 'stuff' he or she is made of, the inner reality in which thoughts, speech, decisions, behavior, and relations are rooted."[3]

Perhaps you hear things like, "Your daughter is a hard worker and so pleasant. What a joy!" Or, "Your son is learning to be less competitive and kinder to children less skilled than him. I'm encouraged for him!" Or maybe you don't hear comments like these but wish you would. Character change is possible!

Connected Qualities

When you think of character, you probably think of individual qualities (e.g., patience, loyalty, dependability, sincerity). This makes sense. Character traits are connected, though. They influence each other and don't work alone.

Having a "web of traits" provides your children with a firm foundation. This foundation may mean that over time your children may be more characterized by obedience than sin. Like the chocolate layer of my mom's dream bars needs the first firm layer of flour, brown sugar, and butter, your children need a foundation. For example, respect for others motivates compassion, caring drives service, and cooperation increases attentiveness. Confident children can be brave. And if you want to prioritize forgiveness, you'll also need to talk about remorse. Joy and gratitude feed off of each other. I could list many other combinations!

Look for character combinations in your life. Begin to realize when one character choice leads to another and then another. When you're struggling and need to make changes, think about more than one quality to use. This will make success more likely than if you start and stick with just one. Seeing how these ideas work for you will make it easier to use them with your children.

Character qualities provide a brick-by-brick foundation for a life well lived. Can you picture it? When character is wide and long and high and deep, it will take a lot to knock it or your children down. Most negative influences won't easily destroy children's character or push them off course. They may be entitled instead of grateful for a while, or impulsive rather than self-controlled. But the entirety of children's character or actions won't be rocked when they can use many connected traits.

Begin to realize when one character choice leads to another and then another.

To help you as you go through the book and then apply the principles, I include a list of forty-eight key character qualities (see the appendix). Focusing on these will be good for your children. I don't want you to be overwhelmed, and the reality that traits are connected means others will naturally develop. Also, you'll see that I list negative examples of the traits (e.g., harsh, cruel, unkind, and aggressive instead of gentle). Sometimes children's unhealthy choices and behaviors make it easier for you to see which positive quality to emphasize.

WHAT YOU WANT

I imagine you have goals regarding your children's character, or you wouldn't be reading this book. You might have more goals for their obedience. That's okay. As I'll address, they're related. Let me share here what can happen when you intentionally teach positive character. I hope you'll be encouraged! I'll follow this with a look at character in general, and then the specific biblical character that I pray you'll want your children to embrace.

Use Complete, Positive Character

Children can be marked by a solid, complete character of positive qualities they consistently use. Developing a reputation based on character is so much better than one based on popularity, beauty, and even ability. These things can come and go or fade entirely. Children's character will shape them when they're taught how to be who they can be. They'll want to be who they are made to be.

Developing a reputation based on character is so much better than one based on beauty, popularity, and even ability.

You don't want children to get into character as if they won a part in a play and must pretend to be someone they're not—angry when they're joyful or mean-spirited when they're kind. You want them to know who they are and trust you with their authentic selves.

I'm confident you want your children to have good character. Let me suggest that *using* good character is a better goal. Using their character allows them to glorify God, positively influence people and culture, and increase their contentment and success. The goal of good character is not that they're known as "good people," even though that can happen. The goal of character is to have influence and impact. Character is active. It is not something to just have. It's something to use.

Children Can Do What's Right

Children can learn right from wrong and when and why to use different character traits to behave in certain ways. They can learn what to do (e.g., be honest), want to do it, and be willing to do it. All three matter! Too many children and adults know what to do, but don't want to do it. They have to be bribed, threatened, and watched. It's exhausting! They're not living up to their potential and they're dishonoring you.

To develop both their head and heart, you'll need to parent differently. When you teach, motivate, and inspire through your example, character, words, instruction, feedback, and attitudes, your children will have both skill and will. Now they'll know what to do (persevere), want to do it (apply themselves even though the task is difficult), and be willing to do it (even if others finish first or they get teased for taking so long). They'll put others first, sacrifice, protect, care, and be able to think of the big picture. These children have the skill and will to be good!

As motivated as your children may be to want to do the right things, they won't always be successful. They're children without lots of experiences. Qualities like self-respect, self-control, respect for others, and effort must be consistently strong to support all their "being able to" and "wanting to" and "willing to." Otherwise, they may become discouraged.

You've lived life long enough to know that on our own efforts, we'll never overcome our sin nature. I praise God that we can mature and make progress. We may demonstrate mature character with one person, but not another. At one meeting, but not the next. How much more might our children struggle with inconsistencies because of fewer positive experiences?

As great as having mature character can be, without the leading of the Holy Spirit, we and our children will fall short. An authentic salvation experience that results in solid motivation to become like

Jesus and an ability and desire to follow the Spirit will change us and our children.

Children Can *Want* to Be Good

When children realize they *can* be good, they may *want* to be good. This is ideal! Their attitudes will make everything easier and both character and obedience will be more likely. Some children tell me they don't want to whine, talk back, or throw temper tantrums. They don't want to cheat, be irresponsible, or treat people unfairly. Many want to be good! These children will be open to your teaching and correction.

Wishing that children will care about being good doesn't work. Complaining that they don't care doesn't help.

Wishing that children will care about being good doesn't work. Complaining that they don't care doesn't help—praying helps! And, with the correct teaching, motivation, and inspiration, your children can develop healthy character. They can care about being good! These children will embrace important qualities. Motivation will be easier. The consequences you put in place for right and wrong choices will be more effective.

. . . Even If the Burden Is Heavy

Let's keep going. Your children can learn to do what's right even when the burden is heavy and their positive actions may cost them something. For example, they can answer questions in Sunday school, even if others tease them. They can willingly stop bullies, even though they realize they might be bullied next. They might help an older person, even if friends laugh at them for doing so. Being right and doing right is worth it to them. They'll handle the burden.

. . . And Even If No One Is Watching

There's more great news. Effective teaching can cause children to do what's right even when no one is watching. You won't have to be a full-time spy. Your children won't behave well only to earn a reward or to avoid punishment. Therefore, you won't always have to be present. They can learn to discern how they're doing. Their self-awareness means they can be appropriately independent. This freedom is beautiful for everyone.

All of the above will most likely mark your children when you raise them with biblical character. Indeed, strong, positive, complete character is better than weak, negative, and incomplete character. Yet, being empowered by love for God, the leading of the Holy Spirit, and truth will take your children so much further. I'm looking forward to your learning about this perspective below.

WHAT IS A "BIBLICAL CHARACTER"?

Parenting differently so children develop biblical character will be worth it. Such a commitment can result in so much good! Reading the definition will show you why.

Biblical character is based on righteous qualities, virtuous standards, and irrefutable principles found in the Bible. This includes, but isn't limited to, how Jesus Christ lived His life.[4] It's also based upon God's ways and will as taught in both the Old and New Testaments.[5] Biblical character marks us when we are humbly obedient to the Bible's truth,[6] discipled to trust Jesus as Savior *and* Lord,[7] forgive and ask to be forgiven when we sin,[8] conformed into the image of Christ through the work of the Holy Spirit,[9] and aim to please, love, and glorify God.[10] Biblical character is perfected as we develop a biblical worldview and our faith, love, wisdom, and obedience matures.

Read that definition again. Allow me to suggest that parenting so biblical character is established will be among your greatest accomplishments as a parent. This can change the trajectory of your children's lives! It can be an ultimate goal. This won't happen overnight, because learning character is a process. Younger children or older children who are new to discussions about God may live out parts of the definition before others. They'll be influenced by the example of your life before them, as well as your teaching.

The Best Part

When you intentionally teach and live out biblical character before your children, they're more likely to fully embrace it. You'll make God attractive and living for Him the best! Now, your children's love for God can compel them to want and use excellent character. They can focus on being obedient to please and glorify God rather than to earn a reward or to avoid punishment. Not depending on someone watching them constantly will mature and free them.

That's not all. When children trust Christ as their Savior, everything changes for them. Everything! I remember when I began to transition to this understanding. Because of one particular pastor, I understood that Jesus didn't just want me to live in heaven with Him forever. Yes, He was my Savior, but He took my sin upon Himself so that I could also live an abundant life *now*, with Him on earth. This is how "heaven comes down."[11] You don't have to do this alone! Involve your pastors, leaders, and friends, especially those your children respect.

Of course, salvation also results in us receiving God's generous gift of the Holy Spirit. Your children can learn to be led by Him. Now they don't have to try to be good on their own, which is impossible![12]

You might be familiar with everything I've written above. That's great! Now I'm asking you to see the relevance of your children's relationship with the triune God to their character. God doesn't just care about their eternal life. He cares about their lives now. Using biblical character will add to their abundant lives! You can parent differently so children develop biblical character. This will leave an undeniable mark!

STANDARDS: GOOD, BETTER, AND BEST

You need to decide what standards you'll raise your children with. Standards set expectations and determine what is good, better, and best.[13] They'll determine which character qualities you'll embrace. And because character determines destiny, your standards will determine who your children become and what they accomplish.

You can think in terms of legal standards enforced by a government entity. I might suggest that people who follow these standards are just getting by. They follow rules and may not think about much else. You could choose moral and ethical standards that are based on societal norms. People who follow these standards won't do something they disagree with even if it is legal. They're typically good people. But there's more.

I'm proud of you for being interested in biblical standards. A biblical character marks you for Jesus! This character allows you to live abundantly.[14] As my friend Lee Nienhuis states, "There is a standard of character we are looking for, and it is found in the heavenly Father. The transformation we are longing for in our society, world, and homes is possible when we yield to God's Spirit. This carving of our character and that of our children is really all about living in the way of Jesus, being conformed to His image— thinking the way He thinks, serving those He would serve, and loving the way He loves."[15]

BELIEFS CAUSE BEHAVIOR

For your children to develop biblical character, you need to pay attention to and address what they believe. I've been teaching that beliefs cause behavior for years. It's a helpful principle! Keep it in mind while you observe your children in light of what you read.

For instance, if your children are impatient, you can declare, "Be patient!" all day long without having a noticeable effect on their behavior. Being told what to do isn't enough. Patience may not be their most important concern. Figuring out what's causing their impatience may be.

Maybe jealousy prevents them from being patient with a sister. They believe you treated her better than you treated them. They believe all siblings should be treated the same or that they should be treated better than their siblings. Their belief and frustration resulted in impatience.

Or maybe children were impatient with their grandparents because they were self-centered. The belief that they're more important or their needs matter more caused them to treat their grandparent inappropriately and unkindly. Teach them why these aren't true beliefs, replace lies with truth, and teach them why and how to be respectful and other-centered. You will discover your children are capable of patience.

To have a lasting influence on children's behavior and choices, including their impatience, look below the surface. Deal with their beliefs so changes in character can occur. Ask God to help you identify beliefs driving your children's behavior. You can ask them, "Why did you do that?" but most children will stare into space and mumble, "I don't know." You can help them figure it out. Long-lasting changes depend on this.

What Beliefs Matter Most?

The most important beliefs are those that will allow your children to develop biblical character. For example, they must believe in the triune God, and in what God, Jesus, and the Holy Spirit has done for them, can do for them, and will do for them. They need to believe that committing to live for Him and putting Him and His ways first is wise.

Your children need to know God is on their side, has the power to protect them, and has equipped them to do great work. They need to believe they can do much for God and that being marked as a follower of Christ is the very best mark of all. Children also need to believe they can and should do the right things right. They need to believe that being good is important and worthwhile, even if it costs them something.

The role of beliefs is such an important concept that I devote chapter 6 to fundamental beliefs and how to change them when necessary. I'm introducing the idea now so you can keep reading with this concept in mind. The longest-lasting changes in your children's character will happen when they believe what best supports the choices and decisions they need to make.

Your children need to know that God is on their side, has the power to protect them, and has equipped them to do great work.

IS CHARACTER REALLY A BIG DEAL?

Character is pervasive, controlling, and leading. This is true whether character is healthy or unhealthy. It can be positive when you thoughtfully and strategically teach good qualities and help children successfully use them across situations with anyone (school, church, job, family, friends, strangers). Character marks us because it forms the foundation of all decisions, choices, attitudes, and actions.

Think about your day and which qualities influenced you. Taking initiative? Being aggressive? Generous? Unsociable? Consistent? Unreliable? Connecting the type of day you've had to your character choices will show you how important it is to prioritize character in your parenting.

For example, my grandma nicknamed me Chatty Kathy when I was very young. My parents raised my brother, Dave, and me to speak respectfully and to listen. If they hadn't done so, I could have become a good gossip. Teasing, impressing with my words, and needing to have the last word could have been my future. I wouldn't have seen anything wrong in using all my words in unhealthy ways.

Dave and I don't remember lessons about speaking, listening, respect, and other qualities. But we knew character was significant and that putting others first was correct. Our grandfather was our city's mayor and our mom and dad were leaders in different organizations.

My parents didn't rely just on the modeling they, our grandparents, and others provided. Positive experiences and proper expectations mattered too. My parents enrolled me in children's theater when I was about ten. And because of their encouragement, I joined the speech team in high school. I wasn't raised hearing, "Be quiet! Be quiet!" Instead, I was given opportunities to use my strengths in healthy ways and to develop mature character.

Because of my background, I became a teacher, coach, earned a PhD in reading and educational psychology, and was a school board member and professor. My parents would want me to mention that they weren't perfect. But it's because of how I was raised and the strength and purpose God provides that I am a Christ follower, founder of a ministry, author, and public speaker today. My brother, Dave, also has strong faith. He was an honoring son and is a wonderful husband, father, grandfather, and brother who also contributes significantly to his profession.

The Impact of Cultivating Character

How we're raised influences more than education and career. For example, solid friendships were only possible for me with the boundaries and guidance my parents and others provided. Picture what might have happened if I had needed to talk all the time and used words in unhealthy ways. Still today, I look for wise ways to use my character and abilities. I'm not always successful, so I'm grateful for family, friends, and colleagues who have wisdom, truth, grace, and mercy. They help me and I want that, because character is destiny!

With a positive character, children are more likely to become who God created them to be. He intentionally, strategically, and personally chose children's gifts, talents, interests, challenges, families, and more.[16] Immature character robs children of their present and future. That's a big deal! They may drop out of school, experiment with drugs and alcohol, question their identity, or become abusive, apathetic, suicidal—the list goes on.

Furthermore, mature character results in fulfillment, joy, peace, gratitude, productivity, contentment, and freedom. It

God intentionally, strategically, and personally chose children's gifts, talents, challenges, and more.

means children are less likely to lie to impress, hide from hard things, or behave one way for one group of people and a different way with others. They're more likely to be blessed, successful, confident, and grow in wisdom and healthy relationships. And, of course, if they're Christ followers, it will be easier for them to display the character of Christ. They hold His reputation in their hands. (So do we!)

Healthy character means children can already begin fulfilling God's purposes for them—to leave the world a better place. They'll be able to engage with others to solve problems. They'll want to be influential! They'll want to influence culture positively! Character for the sake of self isn't compelling. Character for others is.

The healthiest and most mature children are not just confident in themselves or you. They'll also develop confidence in God as you teach them who He is and how He is involved in their lives. Teach them they can trust His wisdom, love, leading, sovereignty, grace, and everything else. They can trust that God created them with good gifts to use and so much more.[17] He is the source of all we are. Make sure you teach and model this.

QUESTIONS TO CONSIDER

1. Do you believe your life would be different if your parents had strategically thought about developing your character? How? Or, if they were thoughtful, how can you thank and honor them?

2. What could you do with your children to help them understand that our character marks us? You could buy wax and seals with your children's initials. Allow them to use them when sending letters and making decorations. You could talk about permanent and erasable markers. You could cut designs in potatoes, apples, or clay. What can you think of?

3. Reread the definition of biblical character. Which elements seem most important to solidify now?

4. Although you may change your mind as you keep reading, choose a few character qualities from the appendix that you want to prioritize for yourself and some you want to prioritize for your children. Keep these in mind as you read.

"This is the one to whom I will look:
he who is humble and contrite in spirit
and trembles at my word."
Isaiah 66:2

How Do Children DEVELOP Mature Character to AFFECT Culture?

B ecause I speak at conventions and for schools, churches, and ministries, I fly a lot, rent many cars, and stay in many hotel rooms. I'm not tired of it because when God called me to my ministry, He called me to all of it. It's not always fun, and travel can be exhausting, but it's always worth it.

I own a car that's perfect for me, but it's older than cars I rent. I'm sometimes surprised by features in newer cars. For instance, I was recently quite confused and distracted by how a rental car's lights worked. I didn't realize newer cars have sensors that allow the lights to adjust automatically to the bright level and then back again. I kept trying to control them.

The same thing happened with the wipers. Technology is always changing, but I had no idea the windshield can now sense when wipers are necessary. I wanted to turn off the intermittent wipers because I didn't think they were required. But I couldn't.

Technology has made many things easier, and we all benefit. As an author, believe me when I say I like the "undo" button that's a part of my word-processing program. We all benefit from devices' reboot features and talk-to-text capabilities. Streaming and GPS may be among your favorite aspects.

Remember that you and your children don't come with technology's features built in. Change isn't automatic. Neither is growth. Maturity will happen because you and your children learn from your experiences, accept and even seek feedback, want to improve, and work at it. When you parent differently, your children have a chance to learn differently.

FORMING A HABIT

Developing character won't happen overnight. Rather, it's a process. Think about yourself. It takes no thought to apply the character qualities you have been using a long time. But, when the Holy Spirit or friends and family prompt you to want to make changes, you'll have to decide if they're right, think about whether the change is worth the effort, and learn how to behave in this new way. It may take some work, but that's normal. As you use the desired quality, you'll gain ability. Then, with continued opportunities, it will begin to define you. The new mark will be evident to others.

When children have to decide whether to lie or to tell the truth, they can choose to be honest. When this works well for them, they'll keep choosing honesty over lying. Honesty becomes a learned ability through repetition and positive consequences, including your affirmation. Honesty then becomes a natural and automatic choice. When children repeatedly make the same choice, a habit forms. Children don't even think, *Should I lie or tell the truth?* Honesty is their choice and it marks them. Being able to add this trait to others they use matures them.

This is how all learning occurs. Children learn to read by reading. They learn to pass the football by passing it. Their confidence increases for music competitions as they compete. In the same way, children's character grows and is strengthened when we expect them to use it and they do.

Start Now

How old should a child be to learn these qualities? The earlier you take character development seriously, the better. Observing young children makes it clear that they're capable of developing healthy and unhealthy character. For example, the sixteen-month-old granddaughter of a friend of mine is already helpful, serving, and other-centered. She throws things away in the trash and wipes her high chair tray without being told. She isn't ready for a discussion about helping others, but she likes being praised and thanked when she does so she knows it's important.

As with anything, it's best if children never develop bad habits. For example, if they're allowed to grow an attitude of entitlement, gratitude won't automatically happen. They'll have to work to forsake entitlement for gratitude. In the same way, learning to be responsible will take longer if they are allowed to be irresponsible. Be alert to children's choices and work so bad habits aren't established.

What examples of this principle can you think of because you've seen the reality in your life or your children's? I think of my coaching days. I coached basketball for fifth- and sixth-grade girls at the same elementary school where I taught second graders. It was mostly just for fun. Teams played against each other in our gym, but never traveled or competed against others. I was glad because this allowed me to teach skills and emphasize technique rather than competing and winning.

Some might say coaching these young girls was challenging because they didn't know much. Actually, it was easy because they didn't know much. I appreciated that I didn't have to help them unlearn ways of dribbling, shooting, passing, or guarding that I didn't think were best. I didn't have to reteach because most girls were inexperienced. Starting from scratch worked well.

These athletes didn't have reasons to doubt me and my ideas.

They were more optimistic and didn't constantly compare my coaching to someone else's. Teaching from nothing is easier than teaching from a bad foundation.

MARKED BY MATURE CHARACTER

It's not enough to say, "My child has character." All kids do. What adjectives would you use to describe your children's character? Mature? Immature? Healthy? Unhealthy? Complete? Growing? Biblical?

As I've explained, character marks everyone. It's a part of our reputation. Most children (and adults) display some positive character qualities and some negative. They may be selfish, but also kind. Stingy, but also generous with some people. Responsible, but sometimes lazy.

Three factors can help you judge how mature your children's character is. First, examine how *complete* their character is and if they use more positive qualities than negative—agreeable versus disagreeable, self-controlled versus impulsive, optimistic versus pessimistic.

Most children and adults display some positive character qualities and some negative.

Maturity also includes how *consistently* children use positive qualities. Are they always, frequently, or rarely submissive? Diligent? Resilient?

Also, how *automatically* do they use the traits? Do they need to be retaught or reminded to use some? Are some automatically used when you're not watching?

To mature children's character, be alert to which traits you model consistently for your children and which ones you don't. Which ones do you need to talk about, teach, correct, compliment, and reteach? And pray! Your children can be truly marked by their character. It can be who they are and not just what they do.

Mature character will develop when you intentionally prioritize it. This is parenting differently! You can do this!

MARKED BY BIBLICAL CHARACTER

Everything I wrote above is also relevant for helping children develop biblical character. What will you need to add to your arsenal so your children will want to use a biblical character and will be able to do so?

The first thing I have to mention isn't a thing, and it's not something you add, but Someone your children choose or who chooses them. An interest in God and pursuing His ways that result in a life-saving personal relationship with Christ by faith in God will significantly influence your children's character. Then as you and maybe others disciple them, they'll grow as Christ did "in wisdom and in stature and in favor with God and all the people."[1] Their character will become more biblical when Jesus becomes the Lord of their thoughts, feelings, choices, and decisions.

The Holy Spirit will help them. He is the closest thing you and your children have to a sensor like my rental car had. He is available to those who have trusted in Christ for their salvation. He is a powerful advocate and much better than a sensor on any car. He makes us holy, guides us to truth, dwells in us, and teaches, helps, counsels, convicts, empowers, gifts, seals, and intercedes.[2] When you and your children know the Spirit and gain experience in hearing and following His voice, discernment and obedience can follow.

Returning to the definition in chapter 1 reveals what else will mark you and your children as having biblical character. Chapters 7 and 8 are full of ideas for how to develop this, but I'll mention a few things now so you can start thinking about how you're doing in this area. For example, you'll want to read Scripture with them, use it in your parenting, point out Bible heroes, and study missionaries as examples of living sacrificially for Christ. You'll want to pray together, teach them how to pray on their own, and talk about how God answers prayers. Other relational activities (i.e., Christian disciplines) like worship, church attendance, and service are also very relevant.

MARKED BY THE BIG THREE

Get ready to be encouraged! When you parent so children are marked by three special character traits, most will want to do what's right and be willing to do it even when the burden is heavy and no one is watching. If you were encouraged thinking about these possibilities when reading the last chapter, here's the rest of the story. Also, as I'll address later, these three cause other qualities to be valuable and lived out.

As I explain in chapters 4 and 5, you'll decide to prioritize certain qualities over others for different reasons. No matter your circumstances, you will want to choose these three. They pay great dividends for mature character and first-time obedience.[3] Emphasize them!

- Gratitude—consistent thankfulness. Not circumstantial gratitude or entitlement.
- Joy—consistent joy. Not circumstantial happiness or joy based on comparisons with others.
- Self-efficacy—having skills to accomplish their goals and believing they can be effective.[4] Not believing they don't have a purpose or can't accomplish anything.

Introduce gratitude, joy, and self-efficacy early and reinforce and reteach them often over time. Be strong. Even if your children declare that everyone else has what they want and they whine, "I need it!" don't give in to their entitlement attitudes. Don't be persuaded by children or the culture that happiness is more important than joy. And, don't do everything for children. If you do, they may conclude they can't do anything for themselves. Or even if they can, they may decide they don't need to. Don't give in to children's apathy or complaining. Do parent differently! Your children will have strong and healthy character. And as you'll see in the next chapter, they'll also be more obedient.

Stop and think. Do these three qualities make sense? Think about yourself first. Can you see that when your character is marked by consistent gratitude, consistent joy, and consistent self-efficacy, you will want to *learn* how to use character qualities? Also, you'll *want* to use them, and you'll be *willing* to use them even when the burden is heavy and no one is watching. You'll most likely be optimistic, positive, and other-centered. You will be willing to be good! If you're treated badly, gratitude and joy will help you bounce back quickly. They'll cause resiliency. Now watch for this process to occur for your children.

Technology's Influence

Teaching these three qualities is imperative because, as I explain in *Screens and Teens*,[5] technology can rob young people and even us of all three. Children can believe happiness is always a realistic expectation. For example, they multitask when they're bored, only download the apps they want, and can be entertained constantly. They listen to the music they want to and talk with the people they want to. Sadly, they think happiness is better than joy.

Children can also become entitled rather than grateful. They have access to so much! They can think they're the center of their universe and everything is about them. Also, because tech makes everything easier, they can downplay the need to learn skills so they can be effective. If ideas or answers don't come to them immediately, they may give up and expect you to do things for them. (I'll come back to the topic of technology in chapter 4.)

CULTURE MARKS US TOO

As I explain in chapter 1, character is something we use, not something we have. Therefore, children will take your instruction about character seriously when they see reasons to develop it. How could they use their character? Without reasons, they won't care and all your teaching and complaining will fall on deaf ears. Or, they may care, but only so they become known as good people. This self-centered and sad motivation will increase pride. Changing culture can cause them to care.

Culture and Your Responsibilities

Perhaps wanting to influence the culture motivated you to pick up this book. I pray that reading this section and the whole book increases your optimism. Maybe you're already doing some things or maybe you want to. Good for you!

You may think loving your family well, praying for leaders, and being involved in your community aren't making a difference. But how much worse would things be if you weren't doing what you're doing? I'm grateful you know that something is better than nothing!

I recently started a new routine to help my voice stay strong. As a public speaker, my voice is my livelihood. Laryngitis and lots of coughing make teaching, podcasting, and radio interviews almost impossible. I added a new supplement because a cheer coach friend recommended it. After my first events using it, a colleague wanted to know what I thought. Of course, I had to say I didn't struggle much, but there's no direct comparison because I'll never speak those exact events without using the supplement. I choose to assume it's helpful. Sometimes we just have to believe we're doing what we can and that it's good.

Changing culture is about more than just what you can do. It's about who you are.

But changing culture is about more than just what you can do. It's about who you are. James Q. Wilson was right when he declared, "In the long run, the public interest depends on private virtue."[6] God will use your character to change culture. The same thing is true for your children. You don't necessarily need a skill set (although you have one) or experiences. Character changes culture!

My friends John Stonestreet and Brett Kunkle write, "How humans and human life are understood, valued, and treated are critical indicators of a culture's health."[7] Are you moaning now? Our culture isn't healthy! Abortion, abuse, trafficking, suicide, bullying, foster children who age-out of the system and often don't do well, homelessness, hunger, scandals, school dropout rates, cutting, drugs, alcohol, sexual promiscuity, gender identity confusion, family dysfunction, mental health crises, generational disrespect and disagreements, apathy, hate, racism—every one of these troubling issues has its roots in people's character. That's where solutions are too.

What Is Normal?

Even as I wrote that long list, another conclusion in *A Practical Guide to Culture* was on my mind: "Culture's greatest influence is in what it presents as being normal."[8] Because it's the ideas in culture that shape us, imagine if we could all agree on answers to questions suggested by Stonestreet and Kunkle: What is true? What is good? What is worthy of our love and devotion?[9]

The lack of agreement on what is normal helps us understand some of today's chaos and tension. For instance, even in the church, not everyone agrees that abortion is wrong. Many boldly attempt to persuade others that their position is not just best, but right. Others argue and waste time putting people down. But, as Stonestreet and Kunkle point out, "If we see people as culture and culture as the enemy we'll likely see people as the enemy and confuse their bad ideas with evil intentions. But culture is not people; culture is what people *do* as people."[10]

The Bible as Our Standard

When you and your children use the Bible as the standard for your beliefs and ideas, you can do the right things right. That sounds arrogant, but we don't need to apologize for believing God knows what's best and has our best interests in mind. Acting on these truths, not just believing the truths, allows you and your children to be agents of change.

Biblical character establishes a firm foundation that allows you to right your part of the world. When we each do our part, little by little, culture changes. Those choices—what you and your children do in the world—change culture.[11] First, consider what this means for your family. As my friend Kayla frequently reminds herself, *Just make the next good choice.* With six young children, including one with special needs, this is how she and her husband prevent being overwhelmed. Then there's your neighborhood and the culture of your son's Little League team. Your daughter's homeschool cooperative. Children's church. The family your daughter babysits for. The fast-food restaurant where your son works . . .

You may be overwhelmed when you think about how big the cultural chaos is. Start with your family. Positively influence the culture of your home, the ideas believed and elevated there, and the influence won't stop there. As I concluded in *Screens and Teens,* "The culture at large may not have any consensus on what's right and wrong, but your family culture can provide that crucial moral compass for your teens."[12]

Of course, there's nothing wrong with aiming big too! Especially believers in the God of the Bible want to see His kingdom come down to earth.[13] That would be the ultimate culture change! Culture is affected when we take our relationships and opportunities seriously and do what we can. That's why I wrote this book. I pray you're inspired, motivated, and equipped to be who you need to be, do what you can do, and help your children be and do the same.

Children Can Change Culture

I don't believe we should throw children to the wolves (expect them to change culture without being discipled) but I do believe you can parent them differently so they can change culture. They'll want to. They'll watch you do it and want to follow in your footsteps. This is part of what it means to parent differently.

Children will especially be agents of change when marked by complete and positive biblical character they consistently and easily use. This means they are taught, motivated, and inspired—by you! They'll be leaders who are able to bear the burden of standing out for God's glory and other people's good.

These children will influence their peer group and others *now*. They may serve on committees or teams at school and church. They may volunteer, do well in their first job, responsibly run errands for you after earning their driver's license, and practice the piano well without complaining, positively affecting your home's culture and their teachers' lives. They'll raise money for important causes and more willingly serve with you when a cause matters to you. They may independently study and earn excellent grades because they have a vision for their future and are already investing in life beyond school.

Some children may develop biblical character, but appear not to use it in significant ways now. Yet they have positive influence in the locker room by just being there. Their presence calms children new to children's church. They are coachable when playing soccer, so other athletes listen better. Because they're known not to cheat and many peers admire them, fewer peers in math class will take this lazy way out. Children marked by biblical character who are willing to be good *are* using their character now to change culture. Let your children know that these effects are huge!

WHAT THIS LOOKS LIKE

Chapters 7 and 8 are all about how to teach character traits, but an example now will be helpful. Children discover and master new traits as you introduce them, model them, teach them, talk about them, and compliment and correct their use. For example, maybe you noticed your children not being grateful when you thought they would have been. Therefore, you choose to prioritize gratitude. You could tell them this is your goal: "Let's learn to be grateful this week. This means we'll notice when someone does something nice for us that we can be thankful for. Then we'll figure out ways to express our gratitude." Or you could decide to *not* announce your objective until there's a teachable moment.

Now you'll need to make time to teach thankfulness like you teach anything else. You can use direct instruction where you sit and explain things like you would if you were teaching math facts. Study relevant Bible verses and introduce children to men and women in Scripture and in life who had much to be grateful for and expressed it. You can also choose to teach conversationally as you're out and about. Among other things, this will depend on your children's ages.

You'll want to include the definition, have children explain gratitude in their words, and share examples from your lives. Because traits are connected, talk about other qualities that make gratefulness more likely. This could include caring about others and being humble, discerning, and generous.

You can contrast gratitude with entitlement and with being thankful only when we're reminded to be. We all tend to learn well through comparisons and contrasts. Have you been to a new restaurant lately? I imagine you compared the service, atmosphere, menu, pricing, and food quality to other restaurants. You might not even plan to do this; it's just natural.

Talk about how it feels to be grateful. Also, share how it feels when someone expresses gratitude for you or something you've done. Notice opportunities for children to be grateful in your family and when you're out and about. Guide them to notice these opportunities too, and ask what they think they could do. Ask if it's sometimes okay to feel grateful and not express it. Why or why not?

When someone has been nice to your children, they might ignore that person like they used to. Or worse, they may act entitled. Maybe these reactions motivated you to prioritize teaching this quality. After you discuss these reactions with your children, they may realize their behavior wasn't right. They'll remember the beauty of thankfulness and consider how they could have expressed gratitude. With more observation and guidance from you that creates positive experiences, your children will become grateful.

Some children will be grateful without any thought, even when facing challenging circumstances. Others may not be. Their ability with gratitude can grow to the point that they'll want to express it. They'll be alert to the opportunities. After a while, you won't need to influence them much, if at all. An attitude of thankfulness will become a part of their character and reputation.

———————

QUESTIONS TO CONSIDER

1. If you've been impatient as your children try to learn new character qualities, what can you do so you remember learning is a process?

2. Do you and your children need to improve the completeness of your character, how consistently you use qualities, or how automatically you use them? You can start now to think about ideas and read for relevant ideas in the upcoming chapters. Why do you believe I included you in this question and didn't make it just about your children?

3. Have you talked with your children much about culture? If you've presented it as only "bad" and they've gotten the impression that they're powerless, how can you start presenting the hope they need to have that, because of their biblical character, they can make a difference? What could you begin doing so you have action and not just words to back up your points?

"Be on guard. Stand firm in the faith. Be courageous. Be strong."
1 Corinthians 16:13 NLT

How Are CHARACTER and OBEDIENCE Connected?

There's more good news about developing character. When we cultivate biblical character qualities, our behavior is transformed—for the good. Consider how Os Guinness states the connection: "Character determines behavior just as behavior demonstrates character."[1]

I remember being excited when I discovered research evidence that joy, gratitude, self-efficacy, and a fourth element I'll explain in this chapter cause children to want to be good even when the burden to do so is heavy and no one is looking. Not only that, this character leads to obedience. But it gets better! These children are capable of and motivated for *first-time* obedience![2] Just the big three plus one!

This mature character results in other-centeredness and agreeable spirits. These children will debate and argue less because they're marked by joy, gratitude, self-efficacy, and more.

Connections between obedience and character were on my mind during a recent trip. I arrived at the airport parking lot I use almost every time I fly and discovered it was closed. I was shocked and unhappy. Fortunately, I arrived in plenty of time, so driving to a different lot wasn't terribly stressful. But it *was* inconvenient.

After parking in the new lot, the shuttle driver met me at my car and drove me to one of the drop-off spots for my terminal. After he pulled away, I discovered that the escalator and elevator that would have taken me to the check-in area weren't working. It was a hundred degrees and I had to walk to the next entrance. To top off my day, just before my flight was supposed to take off, they announced it was delayed. I didn't arrive at my destination until midnight.

Not the day I had hoped for! To behave well when faced with each of these disappointments, I needed to remember what I believe about God, others, and myself. Basing my character and the resulting actions on my beliefs worked. I didn't complain or make employees feel bad, and I did thank the flight attendants when others didn't. (This wasn't about me wanting or needing to be better than anyone. It was about blessing them and, therefore, perhaps helping them.)

Especially when we and our children have solid biblical character, we'll follow a personal standard of behavior regardless of our circumstances. It marks us!

SHOULD YOU PRIORITIZE OBEDIENCE?

All parents desire obedient children. Obedience reaps rewards: children are more secure, family time becomes more enjoyable, and, overall, life is much easier and more fulfilling. But getting to this point isn't easy.

To become obedient, children must understand expectations and learn rules. Many parents assume children will simply "pick up on" expectations. Or they often talk about rules rather than teach children the why and how of following them. Or they explain them once without considering whether the timing is conducive to learning. Reteaching takes initiative and intentionality and may or may not occur. (Of course, some parents teach rules and expectations very well.)

Parents don't always explain exceptions to the rules even though there are times and places when the rules won't be in effect. Maybe they don't want to confuse their children. But not including unique circumstances frustrates children. For example, it helps children when you explain that a rule is not relevant if you have company for dinner. And the opposite may be true. You may set rules only relevant when you have guests in your home.

This reminds me of teaching phonics to the second graders I was privileged to teach. I taught things like, "An 'e' at the end of a word usually makes the first vowel long." And, "When two vowels go together, the first one does the talking and the second one does the walking." Because the "rules" didn't always work, students were frustrated and I'm sure some wondered why I bothered teaching them. (Have you ever noticed that "does" is in the rule and it breaks the rule?!)

Do you feel you're constantly reminding your children of something you believe they should know?

Let me share another issue about teaching obedience I know you're familiar with. Especially with young children and when older ones are learning new rules, you need to be present to reinforce them. If you're not, children will often behave however they want. They may choose only to be good to avoid punishment and to be rewarded. They're not behaving well because these behaviors are a part of them or their values. They're acting well because of you. This means good behavior may not transfer to new situations. Do you feel like you're constantly reminding your children of something you believe they should know?

Simply emphasizing obedience can cause worse character. For example, children may be angry when they're punished, jealous when siblings are rewarded, and sneaky to avoid getting caught. I'm glad you want your children to be obedient. What if emphasizing it isn't the best way to achieve that?

PRIORITIZE CHARACTER!

As I've written, gratitude, joy, and self-efficacy are keys to first-time obedience. And they also give rise to many other character traits.[3] Think about it. When I'm grateful, joyful, and accomplish my goals, I'm more likely to be in the kind of mood that allows me to be obedient. I won't question authority and I'll want to cooperate. Does the same thing happen to you? (Don't stop reading now, but if you did and you chose just to prioritize these three qualities, children would be far ahead of where they are now in character *and* obedience.)

Mature character leads to obedience.

Parenting differently and teaching individual character traits *and* how they're connected increases obedience. Although obedience doesn't guarantee a well-developed character, since obedient children may just be following rules, mature character leads to obedience. It's a richer obedience because it's more heart-centered than rule-based. Children who are taught character traits will know why and how to be obedient. When you also motivate and inspire them, they'll want to be good and they'll know how!

Character's Connection to Disobedience

Character especially helps children become more obedient when you're alert to how they misbehave and you teach related qualities that will help them change. You'll improve at identifying what's most relevant as you read more. You could go to the appendix now while thinking about an obedience issue one of your children is struggling with. You'll be able to identify one or more relevant character traits.

For example, arguing is often related to submission, pride, and selfishness. So rather than constantly declaring, "Stop arguing!" and punishing children when they don't stop, determine which traits they need to learn (e.g., being agreeable, humble, generous). Teach those and eventually, no matter where they are and who they're with, they won't automatically argue. They'll learn to rely on internal strength and remain quiet or bring up ideas with the right attitudes and motivation rather than debating or arguing.

Maybe whining is a relevant issue. It's often related to or caused by fear, jealousy, or disrespect. So, as with arguing, observe what's happening and talk with children if they're old enough. Do they think your expectation is too high and that's why they're fearful? Have you spent more time with one of their siblings and they feel left out? Is their jealousy causing them to whine? Or are they mad at you for some reason and their lack of respect shows up in their complaining?

Of course, there are other reasons your children may whine. Maybe they're confused and that makes them stressed or anxious. That's why they complain in that whiny voice that's so hard for you to hear. What if confusion, too, is rooted in character?

Maybe they didn't listen when you explained something. Did they allow themselves to be distracted? Were they pessimistic from the beginning so confusion was natural? Or did your character choices cause their confusion? Ouch! Were you selfish, which caused you to hurry when explaining something? Did you put your TV show, game, or other needs first?

Can you identify weak character issues in just about every obedience problem? Yes, I think so. Modeling, teaching, and reteaching character will decrease disobedience and increase heart-centered obedience. It's a win-win.

If you're debating me in your mind, you're not the first. You may think my examples are illustrating the need for obedience. There's some truth to that. The question is, what do you teach? Teach character and you get both obedience and character. Teach obedience and you may get neither.

You can probably get children to stop their misbehavior by complaining or yelling. But the changes will often be temporary. And, of course, reacting negatively isn't ideal and you won't feel good about yourself. (We've all done it. Don't look back with shame, look forward with hope. Keep reading!)

If children stop their misbehavior because of what you do rather than because of who they are or who they want to be, they're depending on you. For them to make another right choice, you would have to be with them to monitor their behavior. They'll habitually rely on you rather than themselves or the Holy Spirit. If they keep counting on you, they won't become self-aware. If they're not self-aware, change is unlikely.

ONE MORE THING

Allow me to tell you about a belief system that influences character and obedience. This fascinates me! You will want your children to be God-centered. Yes, being "centered around God" will change them.

Let's first contrast God-centeredness with just knowing about God. That would be my testimony before coming to faith in Christ and even during the first years of my life as a believer. I attended church and loved learning there. I read the Bible, prayed, worshiped, and was genuinely interested in the things associated with my faith. But I admit that I went through the motions and had a check-it-off-the-list mentality. Sadly, I wasn't very open to the Holy Spirit's leading and my pride got in the way. James 2:19 is one of the verses God used to change me. It ends with, "Even the demons believe—and shudder!" I knew I needed to do more than believe!

We can also contrast being God-centered with being self-centered. I'll admit I've lived my life there too. Rather than thinking about God or others, I spent too much time and energy thinking about myself. I wanted to be known and I thought of myself first when making decisions. I'm extremely grateful God grabbed my heart! I can fall back into the old pattern when I'm weak, not in the Word, and not surrounded by good people. This is among the reasons I want you to parent so your children don't embrace deeply rooted negative character traits. It's too easy to revisit them once they've been experienced. I know from experience that self-centered children will not be drawn to positive qualities. Rather, they'd find negative qualities appealing (e.g., disrespectful rather than respectful, resistant rather than flexible, greedy rather than generous, and unhelpful rather than helpful).

Now that we know what God-centered is not, what is it? People centered on God take the spiritual disciplines—or relational activities—such as daily worship, prayer throughout the day, and regular Bible reading—seriously.[4] They don't do them just to do them and they don't do them so they'll feel better about themselves. Rather, they want to be changed by these activities, including service, giving, forgiveness, confession of sin, fasting, communion, rest, and meditation. They do these because they want God to be the center of their lives. He matters to them. They want to become like Him and they will.

God-centered people are more Christlike.[5] Prioritize God-centeredness with the three critical qualities of joy, gratitude, and self-efficacy, and your children won't struggle as much with character or obedience.

"I Get to Go to Church": Believing and Doing

Being God-centered is about doing what Christians do to become who Christians should be. God-centered children (and adults) have a "get to" and not a "have to" attitude toward God.[6] It's a significant foundation for character and obedience because God becomes their strength, source of wisdom, and more. The Holy Spirit will lead, direct, teach, and convict. They'll be optimistic and their attitudes will be more positive.

Think about how to parent your children differently so they move beyond believing they "have to" do everything to them willingly doing things. They will develop God-centeredness:

"I *have* to go to church."

"I *get* to go to church."

"I *want* to go to church."

"I *will* go to church."

"I *did* go to church."

"I *am* a church attender."

Acting in a particular way—in this case, going to church—doesn't automatically result in children with perfect attitudes who consistently attend church. Growth is rarely a simple, clear, linear process. You'll still need to teach and talk with them. There is often much back-and-forth movement between these beliefs. It's a type of chicken-or-the-egg issue.

Children are healthiest when their beliefs drive their behavior—

their being causes their doing. For instance, children who believe church is beneficial want to go to church. Sometimes, though, children (and adults) who don't want to go need to behave as if they want to for beliefs to change. For example, they reluctantly attend church and after a while discover that church can be beneficial. Now, they are "get to" children who move through the beliefs to "I am." Believe this for your children.

Before moving on, I encourage you to go to the church list above and change it in your mind by reading out loud some of these relational activities: reading the Bible, memorizing Scripture, praying, giving, fasting, serving, worshiping, submitting, confessing, and meditating. How might your children word them? For example:

"I *have* to read the Bible again? I just read it yesterday, and Dad read it to us too."

"I *get* to read the Bible. It is cool that I'm learning to read. And Pastor Rick taught us that lots of children don't have Bibles. I guess it's good that I have one."

"I *want* to read the Bible. If I'm honest, Bible verses haven't confused me as much lately. Mom was right. The more I read it, the more I am able to read it."

"I *will* read the Bible. I also realize that the more I read it, the more I want to read it. There are lots of helpful ideas in it. Grandma especially likes it when I tell her what I'm learning."

"I *did* read the Bible. I look forward to reading the Bible now. I did read a pretty long section today!"

"I *am* a Bible reader. And I like it!"

For our children to mature in their relationship with God, be fit for spiritual battle, have a biblical character, and change culture, we must remember that *we do something to become someone.*

One More Thing, Expanded

Let's look at this belief sequence as it relates to chores since they are a relevant obedience and character issue. You will want to move children from the "I have to" attitude of *"I have to do this or I'll be in trouble"* to *"I want to do this because it's right to care about other people. That's part of my commitment as a follower of Jesus."* But that's not all. My joy would be for children to continue through the process to *"I will get up and help now,"* and finally to *"Look, I did it."*

Imagine children moving from a "I have to" belief to "I am . . ." for cleaning their room. They might think these thoughts:

"I *have* to clean my room. There's always so much to do and my parents order me around a lot!"

"I *get* to clean my room. I have my own room! Not all kids do. I'm privileged."

"I *want* to clean my room. Cleaning my room still isn't my favorite thing, but I understand what my parents mean when they talk about taking care of our things."

"I *will* clean my room. I am learning to make time and I discovered I like putting things away."

"I *did* clean my room. I used to waste so much time complaining about cleaning. Now I usually just do it!"

"I have a new identity. I clean my room!"

I realize this has been an ideal description of attitude and belief changes. Very ideal! Many conversations, instruction, and encouragement will need to occur to make each change possible. Struggles and some pushback are normal. I'm sharing the progression and "pretend" thoughts because of feedback I get from parents. Intentionally focusing on specific beliefs and tasks works! Children can learn to cooperate with you and gain independence.

One more thing. Can you see how gratitude, joy, and self-efficacy are foundational to these attitude shifts? And it shouldn't surprise you to realize that when children move from "I have to" to "I am" they have even more gratitude, joy, and self-efficacy. This is another win-win.

QUESTIONS TO CONSIDER

1. In your own words, how can you tell someone about how obedience and character are connected?

2. Review the past week and choose a specific example when your child misbehaved. Could you have decreased his or her misbehavior by emphasizing character qualities? What might you have done differently?

3. Are you where I was in my walk with Christ, doing the Christian relational activities to feel good about yourself and checking them off a list? Would you like to become more God-centered? What might you do first? What about your children?

4. Choose a chore that's a struggle for one or more children and take them through the "I have" to "I am" sequence. What might you discover about their motivation?

"Finally, brothers, whatever is true, whatever is honorable,
whatever is just, whatever is pure, whatever is lovely,
whatever is commendable, if there is any excellence,
if there is anything worthy of praise,
think about these things."
Philippians 4:8

4

What Are Some CORE WAYS to Choose QUALITIES?

Deciding to prioritize character over obedience is just the beginning. Now you need to decide which *specific* qualities to prioritize to help your children build biblical character. Just thinking about character in general terms isn't nearly as effective as reflecting on and choosing certain character qualities.

Think about who you want your children to be. What goals and hopes do you have for them? How do you want them to live their lives? Since character will mark them and is largely responsible for who they become and what they can accomplish, intentional thought about this matters greatly.

You'll emphasize qualities for a long period of time that reflect your family values. You'll begin talking about and teaching these when children are young and continue as they grow. Or because you're learning new ideas, you can start now even if your children aren't young. It's never too late! You can deemphasize these qualities when you see that they've become part of who your children are. Then modeling them and occasionally talking about them should be enough.

In addition, you may prioritize particular attributes for a season because of something a child is going through. For example, if you get a new job or have another baby, you'll want to highlight responsibility. Compassion will help your oldest son if a friend's parents get divorced. If you're frustrated by your children's new, negative behavior, there may be something new going on. Identify it and choose relevant qualities that will help.

How do you choose desirable qualities? You don't have to start from scratch. You can begin with the forty-eight important qualities I've chosen for this book, listed in the appendix.

Based on what I wrote in the last chapter about obedience, you know that parenting differently to prioritize joy, gratitude, and self-efficacy will mark your children well. What else matters? In this chapter, I'll share how you can use children's core needs and three other enlightening systems to decide which character qualities to prioritize. I explain the power and significance of the core needs at a deeper level in my book *Five to Thrive*.[1] I also address them in my other books—that's how important they are![2]

Life is challenging for children who don't have healthy security, identity, belonging, purpose, or competence. These challenges won't just cause problems for children today. They can negatively affect their future. Character qualities will help! Therefore, consider these core needs when choosing which traits to embrace now.

THE PYRAMID EFFECT

As you read about your children's five core needs, picture the needs stacked as a pyramid. How children attempt to meet one core need will affect the others. Security is the foundation and hopefully it's solid. When children don't know who they can trust, and you and others can't trust them, everything else is negatively affected.

Because of the connections among the needs, it was challenging to assign character traits to only one of the needs, as I do below. For example, I could make a case for categorizing integrity and discernment in each need. Still, you'll benefit from seeing what I prioritize for each. It will give you a starting place when you know which core need to shore up. All forty-eight qualities are assigned to at least one core need.

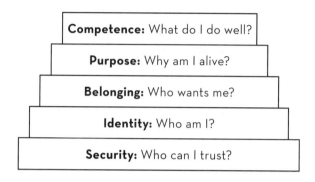

SECURITY: WHO CAN I TRUST?

Without a firm foundation of security in people, children won't have sure footing. They won't grow or achieve as much success because they can't take appropriate risks. They also may be lonely because they don't know who they can trust. These experiences and choices mean they'll experience less, learn less, and even love less.

If they don't value being trustworthy themselves, they may lie and bully more. Because they'll assume people are difficult, they may put their security in things like grades, looks, and popularity. They'll want these things to be dependable, but this isn't wise because they don't last.[3]

Children need to learn who they can trust and how to behave so others can trust them. Therefore, prioritize discernment, forgiveness, honesty, faithfulness, integrity, self-control, consistency, gentleness, kindness, and responsibility.

Think about the current state of your children's security. What qualities might you want to emphasize now?

IDENTITY: WHO AM I?

Children must know who they are. Without this clarity and confidence, they'll be like grains of sifting sand and feathers in the wind. Or worse, they may *intentionally* change to fit in with this or that group. They might pretend not to care about God, and to like a game, movie, or someone's decision about their gender in order to fit in.

Being content in a complete and positive identity and having solid security makes negative identity changes like these less likely. Knowing they can trust themselves and others empowers them to change only for the right reasons. With firm security and healthy identity, rather than compromising truth and values, they'll rest in who they are, find others who like them for who they are, and willingly influence culture.

When character marks children, they'll know who they are and how to behave. This is powerful! You can look at the list of qualities to see which may be relevant to children's identity. If they're not self-aware and have blind spots about who they are, they can be confused, hopeless, or become angry when you try to point things out. In this case, teach about humility, self-respect, and discernment pointed inward to how they feel and outward to how others relate to them. In general, effort and bravery will help them become who they need to be, and generosity, gratitude, sincerity, and unselfishness will serve them well. I would also stress resiliency and remorse, both of which I could have listed as security traits.

Think about the current state of your children's identity. What qualities might you want to emphasize now?

BELONGING: WHO WANTS ME?

Being trustworthy, knowing who they can trust, and knowing who they are form the foundation of a healthy belonging. This is another legitimate need. Without strong connections to family, healthy peers, and adults, children may be lonely and stressed, confused by people, and angry when left out. You've probably seen this play out at times.

Of course, there's no guarantee. The son of friends has healthy security, knows who he is, and has many friends from school and church. Yet, he didn't have friends available to have fun with on the most recent New Year's Eve. Fortunately, Nicole and Eric are aware and involved parents so they can meet part of his need for security and belonging. Because of their relationship, he could admit he was upset and willingly went to dinner and a movie with his mom. Since they often connect through regular dinner and movie "dates," it was easy for her to invite him and not hard for him to say yes. When children meet their needs partly through you, they'll be healthier and more resilient when their first choices don't work out. And, at times, you'll be their first choice!

Resiliency and discernment are essential qualities for belonging. They're genuinely relevant for all five needs. Therefore, I'll elaborate on them even though I have not elaborated much about other qualities I've included. My details may equip you to think well about other qualities.

Discernment helps children know the difference between peers who have a bad day and those who consistently behave in an immature and unhealthy way. For ex-

> *Resiliency and discernment are essential qualities for belonging.*

ample, is Lisa usually kind, cooperative, and gentle, but on one particular day she wasn't? That's different from people who are consistently manipulative and mean. Children need to discern the difference so they know when to maintain a relationship and when to walk away. Discernment allows children to know if they should give someone a second chance. Resiliency is what will enable them to do it.

Discernment is also essential for self-examination. When children struggle with issues related to belonging, they can look back and ask themselves how healthy their security and identity are. You can help them with this analysis. For example, if they're insecure, it's easier to follow the crowd in doing wrong. If their identity is "I must be the best," they'll be prideful and likely relate through competition instead of in healthy ways. They'll be critical of others and impatient and angry with themselves when they're not the best.

What other character traits do you think of for belonging? What strengthens your relationships? Your list might include being agreeable, diligent, loving, forgiving, caring, patient, respectful, fair, peaceful, hospitable, cooperative, and joyful.

Think about the current state of your children's belonging. What qualities might you want to emphasize now?

PURPOSE: WHY AM I ALIVE?

When children don't trust themselves (security), don't have a positive view of who they are (identity), and aren't in life-giving relationships (belonging), they may doubt they have purpose. They won't believe in their todays or tomorrows. They may not persevere to overcome challenges but instead become apathetic and pessimistic. They may never become who God created them to be and that would be disappointing. Tragic, even. Parent differently so this doesn't describe your children!

Children are created on purpose, with purpose, and for a purpose. Therefore, God sets children in relationships where they can serve Him, make Him known, and influence culture. He also gives them the identity He wants them to have. This includes gifts God chose for them, as declared in Ephesians 2:10: "For we are his workmanship, created in Christ Jesus for good works, which God prepared beforehand, that we should walk in them." Because God wants children to fulfill their purpose, He wants children to trust Him, other people, and themselves. If they don't, it's harder to take risks, which is almost always necessary to step out in faith to try new things God has called us to do.

I could have written about the big three—joy, gratitude, and self-efficacy—when addressing any of these core needs. Children who use them are more trustworthy and have a more positive identity and healthier relationships.

Children are created on purpose, with purpose, and for a purpose.

These children are also more able to fulfill their purpose.

Joy and gratitude lead to peace and contentment, which positively affect purpose. These children won't struggle as much with depression or anxiety. These feelings may come and go, but they won't overwhelm or define the children. Therefore, they can believe they have purpose and will be able to focus on it.

Gratitude and joy also make other-centeredness more likely. When this is coupled with self-efficacy (the ability to accomplish their goals), these children will be unstoppable. Knowing they can be effective helps them look for purpose. Expecting to be effective is a huge blessing! Now they just won't be frustrated or angry about the chaotic culture but will want to improve it. They want to because they believe they can. If they couldn't, they'd choose not to be motivated—wanting to change something without real hope that they can is discouraging and demotivating.

Because lack of purpose can cause apathy, despair, isolation, and suicidal thoughts, you'll want to emphasize character qualities such as hope, confidence, and optimism. Others with value include initiative, compassion, other-centeredness, helpfulness, determination, flexibility, submission, and self-efficacy.

Think about the current state of your children's purpose. What qualities might you want to emphasize now?

COMPETENCE: WHAT DO I DO WELL?

When I speak to parents about these five core needs, I realize that many have made competence the foundational first need. They flip the pyramid. I get it. The culture and many organizations celebrate what we do well exclusively. Maybe your parents did that and only paid attention to you when you did things well or perfectly. They may have given you the impression that your performances mattered more than you did. It affected you then and this may affect your parenting now.

If you prioritize your children's competence, you're not alone. But think about it. Without them meeting the first four needs in healthy ways, competence isn't necessary. Maybe you would have said, "Competence isn't possible." That's true too. But, more significantly, if your children don't have healthy security, identity, belonging, and purpose, they don't *need* competence. They don't need to be good at anything without people to serve and purposes to fulfill. And they won't believe they can be good at anything if their identity is rooted in negative qualities and they don't trust themselves.

By parenting differently, you establish the power and health of the first four needs, and your children can develop the competence they need. Like in so much of life, paying attention to the foundation of anything improves everything.

Purpose drives competence. We share some purposes while some are unique. No matter the purpose, character in general will always be everyone's most crucial competence. Our character equips us to be and do so much! We all need competence for at least obedience, love, and learning. Sharing the gospel and discipleship also come to mind. Your daughter may have a unique purpose to earn a part in a theater production. Your son may want to learn to detail cars. They'll work on competence you and I don't need.

Character in general will always be everyone's most crucial competence.

Many of the traits I've highlighted in the other needs are relevant for competence. I'll add these: humility, teachability, decisiveness, carefulness, perseverance, resourcefulness, and initiative.

Think about the current state of your children's competence. What qualities might you want to emphasize now?

WHAT ABOUT YOU?

As you've read, have you thought about whether *your* core needs are healthy? Perhaps go back and reread this section and make it about you this time. The way you do or do not meet your needs affects your character and parenting. Working on yourself while you parent well is a beautiful way to honor your children.

THE BEST ANSWERS TO ALL FIVE QUESTIONS

Family and friends can help you meet these core needs, and we can also do our own work, as I explain in great detail in *Five to Thrive*. I hope you'll take my lists of qualities assigned to each of the needs seriously. Character qualities are a profoundly meaningful way for you and your children to meet each of their needs because character influences your decisions, choices, attitudes, actions, and life's fulfillment. Character is destiny!

As you read, perhaps you thought about how God meets these needs—for you and your children. He definitely wants to! He meets them authentically and permanently when we put our faith in Him and are discipled into more and more love, wisdom, and righteousness.

You and your children will be healthiest and most mature when you personally know, prioritize, believe in, and trust God, Jesus, and the Holy Spirit. This God-centeredness matures you because you know truth, want to glorify God by becoming more like Christ, and have the leading and conviction of the Holy Spirit.[4] You will have dynamic biblical character and you'll want to be good because of how He meets your needs.

CHILDREN'S STRENGTHS: TOO MUCH OF A GOOD THING?

Although strengths are an important part of children's competence, sometimes children's strengths get them into trouble. As I like to say, anything well done, overdone, is badly done. And too much of a good thing isn't a good thing! As I wrote in chapter 1, without boundaries, modeling, and teaching from my parents, my ability with words could have gotten me into major trouble.

Anything well done, overdone, is badly done.

As I address in my book *8 Great Smarts*, you might have children who like to draw so much that they draw when and where they shouldn't. Your children may make noise constantly. Others may ask "Why?" and "Why?" and "Why?" again until you're about to lose your patience (or maybe you already have). If you're raising a child who touches everything, I imagine you're stressed when you're in a museum, your great-aunt's apartment, or a store with valuable items.[5]

Some children are very analytical and need to analyze and understand everything to feel secure. Some are imaginative and want to tell you every long story and idea they have. You may have playful children who have a hard time staying serious and focused for any length of time.[6] Children have many types of strengths and young children especially may need help to use them well. You don't want to tell them "stop" and "no" so often that they stop using them entirely. Therefore, prioritize three key qualities.

- Self-respect because children will want to use their strengths for good and they will value themselves enough to develop and use the other qualities.

- Self-control because they will be able to use their strengths for good.

- Other-centered because they'll use their strengths and qualities to benefit others.

CHILDREN'S NEEDS: PAY ATTENTION

Not only do all children have strengths, they also have issues, challenges, and attitudes that concern you. No matter what qualities you might choose to prioritize, children's behavior and choices may "tell" you to prioritize others. For example, children may be dishonest, pessimistic, or lazy. These traits may temporarily come and go, but can become permanent parts of their immature character if you don't intervene. They need you to pay attention to their needs.

Two negatives that occasionally show up in me and are always signs that there's something wrong are impatience and a critical spirit. I'm grateful for them because they point out a problem I must discover and overcome. Pay attention to children's negatives. Especially when they're unexpected, realize they're teaching you something. Observe to discern their origin so you know what attitudes to talk with children about and which qualities to emphasize.

For instance, if your son suddenly stops cooperating with his siblings, he needs you to prioritize cooperation. Remember, though, character qualities never work alone, and inappropriate behavior and choices are caused by something. Therefore, examine why his character has changed so you know what to address. Is he jealous of someone? Or is he prideful? Does he need to be in charge? The best way to help him become cooperative may be to help him process his jealousy, pride, and need for power.

Also, observe his siblings. Is your son uncooperative because of how *they're* behaving? Maybe an older sibling teased him and another one embarrassed him when he lost a game. Dealing with their choices will allow your son to return to his normal cooperative self.

Has your daughter become careless? Even if it's not on a list of high-priority qualities, you'll want to intervene. What other qualities are related? Is she inattentive because she's self-absorbed? Is she not responsible? When thinking this way, you might discover that being self-absorbed is a more significant issue than carelessness because it's causing her carelessness, inattentiveness, and irresponsibility.

Even if you choose ten or more qualities to prioritize, different attributes may rise to the top for different reasons. You'll be wise to meet these needs so problems don't escalate. What do you currently see that you can talk about and do? Watch for your children's character to mature. Your positive orientation and expectations are a part of how you can parent differently.

What About Special Needs?

If you have children with unique or special needs, perhaps you have thought of them or their siblings as you've been reading. Great! For example, if children are impulsive or have been diagnosed with ADD or ADHD, you may want to prioritize self-control, patience, unselfishness, and being careful. Children on the autism spectrum tend to communicate and relate differently. Therefore, prioritize cooperation, flexibility, hopefulness, and bravery.

If your children have learning needs such as dyslexia or dysgraphia, you may want to.prioritize initiative, optimism, diligence, resiliency, and confidence. What about the opposite? Intellectually gifted children may need to exercise teachability because they may think they know enough (or everything!). Humility, kindness, and compassion also come to mind.

This certainly isn't an exhaustive list, but I hope it's helpful and you're empowered to think about what would be wise for your children. Also, think about siblings of these children. When they're encouraged to understand their sibling, to help and serve, they often develop more mature character than their peers. For example, siblings of a brother or sister diagnosed with oppositional defiant disorder will need to learn kindness, patience, flexibility, and respect. Depending on the issue, emphasizing humility, cooperation, respect, gentleness, and love are always appropriate.

My friends Luke and Caleb, brothers of my friend Abby, learned about sacrifice early. And because they needed to play and learn without direct supervision, especially as their parents went to appointments and helped Abby with therapy because of her Down syndrome, they learned self-control and how to be resourceful. But there was so much more! They're the fine young men they are partly because much was expected from them. Read Julie's recollection of Abby's older and younger brothers and be encouraged if you're raising unique children:

> Caleb and Luke developed diligence as they recognized the need to help us accomplish everyday tasks, especially when things became very challenging and basic survival was our focus. They developed compassion and learned to have compassion for others who struggled. They learned resiliency and saw how we could overcome any obstacle with God's help. They learned discernment and what things were really important.[7]

TECHNOLOGY

Let me close out this chapter by touching on something that can destroy character if you're not careful. You can choose essential qualities and still see little growth in children if they use lots of technology without your guidance. They may not realize how technology influences their character and behavior because most haven't known life without it. But you know its effects, so you know boundaries matter. So does the teaching of certain traits because of what technology does to children's hearts.[8] For example:

- Because tech makes things quick and easy, teach about sacrifice, effort, caring, flexibility, and perseverance.
- Because tech is about them, teach humility, gratitude, selflessness, and other-centeredness.
- Because tech offers so many choices, teach decisiveness, faithfulness, and responsibility.
- Because tech is always with them and makes information easy to find, teach humility, teachability, and respect.

Children may not realize how technology influences their character and behavior because most haven't known life without it.

What can you do? You and your children can use less technology and become more aware of why, when, where, and how you use it.

If children don't have their own devices yet, continue to delay if you can and buy them the right devices when you decide they're ready.[9] For example, because using tech can cause self-centeredness, if children are already showing this trait, the effect of tech could be disastrous. Therefore, you will want to teach about other-centeredness, contrast it with self-centeredness, and tell your children that you expect to see improvement in this area before you will give them a device or allow them to use additional platforms on their device.

QUESTIONS TO CONSIDER

1. Look back. How are core needs relevant to your or your children's struggles? Is improvement in their character and obedience more realistic if you shore up a core need or two? Why? Which ones? How?

2. Think of challenges not directly related to character that children are having. Maybe they're bored in a class, are struggling with new expectations from their piano teacher, or aren't maintaining friendships. Think through how you would benefit from identifying which core need or two are relevant to the issue and then how that helps you identify character qualities to emphasize.

3. Which of your children's strengths or challenges do you see in a new light because of what you've read? How and when can you talk with them to explain what you now understand and how you might talk with them differently?

> "Take hold of my instructions; don't let them go.
> Guard them, for they are the key to life."
> *Proverbs 4:13 NLT*

What BIBLICAL TRUTHS Will Help You Choose QUALITIES?

'm excited about this chapter. That's not to say I'm not grateful for what God has allowed me to share in the others. I am! But this chapter is a key to my philosophy and everything we believe in at Celebrate Kids.

Having the definition of biblical character from chapter 1 in mind as you read will help you. Consider the various ways you can choose which character qualities to emphasize for your children and entire family so their character truly becomes biblical.

GOD'S CHARACTER

Parenting with the goal that your children become more like Christ is essential if you're going to raise them to have biblical character. This transformation is so important to Jesus that He prays this will happen in His High Priestly Prayer recorded in John 17. He asks God to sanctify us—to set us apart by making us holy.[1] On our own, this is impossible. We need Jesus!

I'm encouraged Jesus prays for you and your children, because becoming like Him is a high calling. You need His help to follow these commands:

- Be "imitators of God." (Eph.5:1–2)
- "Walk in the same way he walked." (1 John 2:6)
- "Put on the new self, created after the likeness of God." (Eph. 4:24)
- "Be conformed to the image of his Son." (Rom. 8:29)

Descriptions of God's Character

Studying Christ's character will refresh you and give you much to teach your children. His character has been and always will be the same. If you're going to become like Him, this is a great place to start. Imagine talking with your children about what you learn in these verses about God and how He would want them to behave. Are the qualities here ones you'll emphasize in your children's character development?

- "But the LORD sits enthroned forever; he has established his throne for justice, and he judges the world with righteousness; he judges the peoples with uprightness." (Ps. 9:7–8)

- "Gracious is the LORD, and righteous; our God is merciful." (Ps. 116:5)
- "Oh give thanks to the LORD, for he is good; for his steadfast love endures forever!" (Ps. 118:29)
- "The LORD is gracious and merciful, slow to anger and abounding in steadfast love. The LORD is good to all, and his mercy is over all that he has made." (Ps. 145:8–9)
- "Holy, holy, holy is the LORD of hosts; the whole earth is full of his glory!" (Isa. 6:3)
- "Anyone who does not love does not know God, because God is love." (1 John 4:8)

God's Names

Teaching God's names is an easy way to teach His character. You'll benefit from knowing them too! For example, what do these names tell you about the character of Christ? Can you see yourself challenging your children to behave as He does?

- "For you are my rock and my fortress; and for your name's sake you lead me and guide me." (Ps. 31:3)
- "For to us a child is born, to us a son is given; and the government shall be upon his shoulder, and his name shall be called Wonderful Counselor, Mighty God, Everlasting Father, Prince of Peace." (Isa. 9:6)

- "Behold, the virgin shall conceive and bear a son, and they shall call his name Immanuel." (Matt. 1:23)
- "Again Jesus spoke to them, saying, 'I am the light of the world. Whoever follows me will not walk in darkness, but will have the light of life.'" (John 8:12)
- "My little children, I am writing these things to you so that you may not sin. But if anyone does sin, we have an advocate with the Father, Jesus Christ the righteous." (1 John 2:1)

Christ's Interactions

Studying Christ's words and interactions in the Gospels allows you to see His character in action. For example, He is faithful, compassionate, wise, and forgiving.[2] You and your children could read the Gospels specifically to notice Christ's character. There are many more traits than I just mentioned. For example, among other qualities, you can find evidence He is humble, loving, committed, persevering, gentle, patient, and other-centered. How long will your list be?

Now What?

Take your time with this chapter. To increase biblical character and to instill it in your children, what might you want to learn more about related to God's character, His names, and how Christ interacts? Have you already made some commitments to what's valuable? How will these change you? How will you make sure to follow through?

BIBLE HEROES

God isn't the only One worthy of studying in Scripture. Which men and women included in Scripture have always mattered to you? Whoever you think of, I imagine it's partly because of their character. Let your children know and challenge them to consider who they value and why.

For example, Daniel and Esther were both young, but acted with great maturity. Do you see their courage? Humility? Submission? Faithfulness? What else?

How could you use Moses, Caleb, David, Paul, Job, and Timothy as examples of men with outstanding character that changed culture? What about Mary and Martha, Deborah, Ruth, and Mary, the mother of Jesus?

Be on the lookout for examples of excellent character as you read Scripture. You may want to point out unnamed people, too, like the boy with the fish and bread and the eunuchs who served Esther.[3] People like them can help you reinforce the idea that we don't do what we do to be recognized.

How will you parent differently using Bible heroes? What's important to you?

GOD'S TRUTH

There's much in God's holy Word about His hope for our character. He wants us to live a certain way. Allow me to offer these passages and ideas. You might think of others to study and share with your children. I hope you will!

Micah 6:8

For all God has done, is doing, and will do for us, I don't think God asks too much of us in this verse.

> He has told you, O man, what is good; and what does the LORD require of you but to do justice, and to love kindness, and to walk humbly with your God?

Picture yourself talking with your children about what it means to *do* justice. How would they behave if they *love* kindness? How might you describe what it means to *walk* humbly? If these qualities matter to you, make sure they know why. As I'll address more in chapter 7, you'll want to talk about the qualities, teach them, affirm children when you notice them behaving in these ways, and correct them when they don't.

How will you parent differently knowing this passage?

2 Peter 1:5-8

This is a rich passage that contains quite a challenge. In chapter 1, you might remember that I explained that qualities are connected. When you read the passage and notice this, you'll see there are only eight traits. This passage is a perfect example of this connected principle and offers you a wonderful opportunity to talk with your children about this.

> For this very reason, make every effort to supplement your faith with virtue, and virtue with knowledge, and knowledge with self-control, and self-control with steadfastness, and steadfastness with godliness, and godliness with brotherly affection, and brotherly affection with love. For if these qualities are yours and are increasing, they keep you from being ineffective or unfruitful in the knowledge of our Lord Jesus Christ.

You may want to start by working with your children to define the words. Then ask everyone why they think Peter paired them the way he did. For instance, "brotherly affection" must be different from "love" or they wouldn't both be mentioned. How do they support each other? I've benefited from connecting "steadfastness" to "self-control" as I work on finishing this book. What connections matter most to you or your children now?

Also, take advantage of talking about the phrase "Make every effort to . . ." Always make sure your children know that effort, diligence, and perseverance will be necessary to forsake their sin nature and develop biblical character. What other qualities from the appendix would you connect to "make every effort"? If you pretend developing biblical character is easy and automatic, you'll be frustrated when progress is slow, and your children will be frustrated too. This will rob you and them of all hope and growth.

Take advantage of talking about the phrase "Make every effort to . . ."

How will you parent differently knowing this passage? What's important to you?

The Beatitudes

The Beatitudes are taught in what's known as the Sermon on the Mount. "Beatitude" comes from the Latin word *beatitudo* which means "blessedness." These challenges describe true, blessed disciples—the way to live today and future rewards if we do.

> Seeing the crowds, he [Jesus] went up on the mountain, and when he sat down, his disciples came to him. And he opened his mouth and taught them, saying: "Blessed are the poor in spirit, for theirs is the kingdom of heaven. Blessed are those who mourn, for they shall be comforted. Blessed are the meek, for they shall inherit the earth. Blessed are those who hunger

and thirst for righteousness, for they shall be satisfied. Blessed are the merciful, for they shall receive mercy. Blessed are the pure in heart, for they shall see God. Blessed are the peacemakers, for they shall be called sons of God. Blessed are those who are persecuted for righteousness' sake, for theirs is the kingdom of heaven. Blessed are you when others revile you and persecute you and utter all kinds of evil against you falsely on my account. Rejoice and be glad, for your reward is great in heaven, for so they persecuted the prophets who were before you." (Matt. 5:1–12)

Talk with your children about these qualities, their meanings, and why you believe they're essential. Encourage them by sharing how they have been peacemakers, merciful toward others, and more motivated to be righteous than before. Let your children know you're not the only one who wants them to do what's right even if they pay a cost. God desires this for them!

Also, you might want to take the time to read all of Matthew chapter 5. You'll notice that the Beatitudes are immediately followed by a section in verses 13–16 about being "the salt of the earth" and "the light of the world." Ask your children if they can see reasons Jesus would have taught people how to be blessed before telling them they are salt and light. Make connections for them to their lives. Has their character allowed them to be effective ambassadors for Christ in the past few days? Make sure they know.

Show them they're living out a biblical character!

You could also talk about the significance that Jesus tells them, "*You are* the salt of the earth and the light of the world." It doesn't say they "could be" or "think about whether you'd like to be." He told them, "You are." What a beautiful picture that identity controls behavior. Jesus knows us and He knows who He wants us to be. You and your children can become who you are told you are. Then you can do what God has called you to do. Read that again and parent with this principle in mind. This is parenting differently!

Have you noticed what Jesus teaches about in verses 21–48? Anger, lust, divorce, oaths, retaliation, and loving our enemies. Especially if your children are older, you may want to connect the dots between the Beatitudes and these challenging issues.

How will you parent differently knowing this passage? What's important to you?

Fruit of the Spirit

Knowing Christ's character and wanting to behave like Him are great goals for you and your children. Your Christlike character will be refreshing and can point others to Him. Here's another passage to help you. The fruit of the Spirit is very instructive. Paul contrasts people who easily sin because they're led by the flesh (Gal. 6:19–21) to believers who should be led by the Spirit. This list also captures main attributes of Jesus.

But the fruit of the Spirit is love, joy, peace, patience, kindness, goodness, faithfulness, gentleness, self-control; against such things there is no law. (Gal. 5:22–23)

A genuine salvation experience should result in living out these qualities. Are you and your children known by love and kindness? Can you think of times when you're gentle when others might have been aggressive? Do these choices mark your children? If so, great! Keep up the good work.

Your Christlike character will be refreshing and will point others to Him.

Of course, you can teach each quality before children have a personal relationship with Christ. They won't have the Holy Spirit's help in behaving in these ways, but they can still learn to become more of each one than they currently are.

How will you parent differently knowing this passage? What's important to you?

The "One Anothers"

I've written about and taught about the "one anothers" of the New Testament for several years. They're compelling and so practically helpful, especially because we live, learn, work, and play in community. Getting these right positively affects belonging and the other four core needs since they're all connected.

Because character is something to use for the benefit of others and our culture, the "one anothers" are highly relevant. These qualities will get your children's eyes off themselves, improve relationships, and move them to bless others.

"Love one another" is recorded many times, and one could argue that every "one another" is a way of loving people well. About one-third of the commands are especially related to unity, humility, and encouragement.[4] With your life and teaching, your children can be powerfully and positively marked by unity, humility, and encouragement!

Admonish, agree, bear burdens, bear with, build up, care, comfort, confess sins, do good, encourage, exhort, fellowship with, forgive, greet, honor, live in harmony, live in peace, love, pray, serve, sing with, stir up, submit, teach, wait, wash feet, and welcome.

Be gentle, hospitable, humble, kind, patient, and tenderhearted.

Do not be consumed by others, bite, devour, envy, grumble, hinder, judge, lie, provoke, repay evil for evil, or speak evil against.

How will you parent differently knowing the "one anothers"? What's important to you?

FAMILY VALUES AND YOUR WORLDVIEW

What marks your family? Some may answer "love and concern." Others may realize the truth is "complaining and grumbling." What do you wish marked your family? Of course, understand that wishing it so won't make it so. You need to teach the qualities you value. Choosing qualities and putting a list of them on the refrigerator isn't enough.

It shouldn't surprise you that I believe basing your family values on Scripture is wisest. Be careful that culture doesn't lead you. It would suggest popularity is a significant value. People who value popularity will make changes to stay popular as "what's cool" changes. Or, you may know people who value money. They talk about what they own, the size of their house, and their recent bonus. They make decisions based on money.

Many of us choose life verses or verses for a year. Some choose a word of the year. These influence decisions we make and what we see and think about. The verses and words become very influential in our worldview. But it's a chicken-and-the-egg issue. Unbeknownst to many, their worldview caused them to choose the verses, words, and priorities—like popularity or money.

Summit Ministries, a premier worldview ministry that I love working with, explains the importance of worldview this way: "Worldview matters because it's the lens through which people see the world. Your worldview is an invisible, but very real, filter that you use to understand why things are the way they are. . . . It is what helps us to navigate everyday life. The way we interact with each other, the decisions we make, and the values we hold all flow from our worldview."⁵

Maintaining a *biblical* worldview changes you. This means God's Word and ways are your filter. You value and act upon what He believes and how He would behave if He were here. For example, a biblical worldview will inspire you to know and value truth because Jesus is truth and wants and even expects us to stand for truth. It's why you listen to the people you listen to, have perhaps changed churches, and told children they can't listen to music from a particular artist.

A biblical worldview also influences you to love as God does. Many people love. But believers who hold to a biblical worldview and use God and His Word as their platform and filter will love as God does. Therefore, we'll love people even when we don't love their behavior.

Answering big questions like these will reveal your worldview: Why are we here? What is the meaning and purpose of life? Is there a difference between right and wrong? Is there a God?⁶

In addition to answering those questions, ask yourself what's important to you. What do you value and believe? How do you spend your time, money, and talent? Look at your current character. It, too, will reveal what matters to you.

In chapter 1, I wrote that character is based on beliefs and values. Now you understand more about the values. If your children value people, they'll prioritize respecting others, hospitality, and flexibility. If they value learning, they'll prioritize teachability, initiative, and resiliency. If they value their relationship with you, they'll prioritize submission, politeness, and faithfulness. What they value is influenced by their worldview. Parent differently so values and qualities you prioritize spring from Scripture and a biblical worldview.

A "Life-and-Love Letter from Our Creator"

Because your worldview is your filter for what matters, it's critical to your life and your children. They may value what you value if you teach them *why*. And if you have integrity and live your values in front of them, there's a greater likelihood they'll adopt them as their own. If they see that your filter doesn't work, they won't be interested. Beliefs, behavior, character, choices, decisions, thoughts, and feelings are birthed here, so be careful!

If you want to live for Jesus and you value God and His ways and will, then watch to ensure that is happening. Does your life align with fundamental beliefs related to a biblical

Your children may value what you value if you teach them why.

worldview? For instance, people with a biblical worldview know they were created by a loving God and saved from themselves and reconciled to God by Jesus. They prioritize their relationship with Jesus and invite others to know Him.

Pay attention to your experiences and the experiences your children have because they will influence their worldview. For example, do you remember my friends Caleb and Luke, whose sister Abby has Down syndrome? Because of their experiences with Abby, they developed respect for everyone as part of their world-view. They knew she was an image bearer, created in the image of God, and so was everyone else. Look to create experiences for your children in your church and community so they develop a biblical worldview that will inspire them to change culture.

Of course, reading and studying the Bible is of utmost importance if you and your children will have a biblical worldview. The Bible is the best instruction manual you and your children could ever read. I like to describe it as a life-and-love letter from our Creator.[7]

Perhaps reading a different translation so Scripture comes alive in a new way will invigorate your passion for Scripture. For example, although I have a Bible I use in church and for studying, I enjoy doing my daily reading from the *One Year Chronological Bible*.[8] I began using this Bible off and on about twenty years ago. Now our church reads it together and I enjoy discussing verses and conclusions with a friend. She's never used this translation before so she sees new things even though she's a student of the Word. I'm not surprised. This happens to me too! Expect relevant truths to jump off the page into your heart.

For example, I'll list some of my life and ministry verses that drive my beliefs, character, and choices. If you're not terribly familiar with the Bible, these will demonstrate how practical and uplifting Scripture is! They remind us that God doesn't expect us to live well alone. We don't need to be perfect, because God is full of grace and mercy and sent us Jesus.

- "Be very careful to love the LORD your God." (Josh. 23:11 NLT)
- "Be sure to fear the LORD and serve him faithfully with all your heart. For consider what great things he has done for you." (1 Sam. 12:24)
- "Seek me and live. Seek good, and not evil, that you may live. Hate evil, and love good." (Amos 5:4, 14–15)
- "The LORD gives his people strength. The LORD blesses them with peace." (Ps. 29:11 NLT)
- "The fear of the LORD is the beginning of wisdom." (Prov. 9:10)
- "The reward for humility and fear of the LORD is riches and honor and life." (Prov. 22:4)
- "I, the LORD, have spoken! 'I will bless those who have humble and contrite hearts, who tremble at my word.'" (Isa. 66:2 NLT)
- "I am the Lord, the God of all flesh. Is anything too hard for me?" (Jer. 32:27)
- "But as for me, I will look to the LORD; I will wait for the God of my salvation; my God will hear me." (Mic. 7:7)

- "Be watchful, stand firm in the faith, act like men, be strong. Let all that you do be done in love." (1 Cor.16:13–14)
- "Whoever speaks, as one who speaks oracles of God; whoever serves, as one who serves by the strength that God supplies—in order that in everything God may be glorified through Jesus Christ. To him belong glory and dominion forever and ever. Amen." (1 Peter 4:11)

Be, Do, Have, and Help

When teaching at Summit Ministries, I asked young adults ages sixteen to twenty-five to write down five things they want to be, do, have, and help in their lifetime.[9] It's a quick way for them to discover values they might not even know they hold. You and your children can do this too for the same reason. After a few minutes, I called on a few students to share, and a nineteen-year-old young man volunteered this answer for what he wants to have: "I want enough so I can share with those who don't." I loved his response and it generated a great discussion. Can you see how it's rooted in his worldview—how the world works?

You're a family unit partly so you can pass on what's important to you. Your children are intentionally yours! The right worldview and the values that arise from it will set children on a wise path of confidence and success. But if you want them to adopt and live with and by your values, you'll want to teach them the character traits they need to carry them out.

For example, I imagine this young man's parents have a biblical worldview. Therefore, they parent differently and prioritize what

Your children are intentionally yours!

God would want their children to believe and how He would want them to behave. These parents didn't use their neighbors or others as the standard of what's right. They were generous, other-centered, compassionate, unselfish, and nonjudgmental. This is what God's Word teaches. But I predict they went beyond being these ways and talked about and taught the qualities that led to their son developing a generous spirit.

There's a bit of the chicken-and-the-egg principle here. Values cause character qualities to matter. And character qualities make values compelling and easier to embrace. For instance, you might have a naturally generous daughter. She frequently notices people in need. She gives from her abundance, even when she doesn't have much. God wired her with this gift, so you can celebrate it by making generosity a value for your entire family. Children leading a family is a beautiful thing!

BAKER'S DOZEN

I pray you're encouraged and not overwhelmed. The next two chapters are full of ideas for teaching beliefs and character qualities. Before you turn there, I'll list the top thirteen traits I've chosen based on everything I've written and what I see children struggling with. Let this list guide you if you want. Use those categories to choose what's best for *your* children.

Emphasize the qualities based on God's character and truths if establishing biblical character is most important to you now. Stress your worldview and values if these are new ideas to you. If you hear yourself saying "no" a lot, examine how you're responding to your children's strengths. You get the idea.

Grateful

Joyful

Self-Efficacy

Humble

Resilient

Discerning

Brave

Effort

Compassionate

Generous

Self-Respect

Self-Control

Other-Centeredness

(Respect for Others)

QUESTIONS TO CONSIDER

1. Go back through the chapter—perhaps explaining the different categories to your spouse or someone close to you whose wisdom you value—and decide how to choose character qualities to emphasize. If your children are old enough, possibly involve them in helping you decide. You might be interested in learning what help they think they need. (If you're a single parent, my heart goes out to you. I pray family and friends support you well. You can do this!)

2. How did you respond to all I shared about who God is and who He wants you and your children to be? Think about Him and how you're doing in these areas. What feelings do you have? How could you express your questions and your gratitude to God?

"Keep your heart with all vigilance,
for from it flow the springs of life."
Proverbs 4:23

What Foundational BELIEFS Are ESSENTIAL?

Because of some issues with my left foot, I'm not allowed to walk on a treadmill. Occasionally, my trainer assigns me the task of walking laps instead. While I was working on this chapter, that's exactly what she did. On this particular morning, between the first and second time I walked laps, Brad, another trainer, had a client stretch out on the floor to complete an assigned exercise.

Brad realized I was about to walk in the area, so he pointed out Susan and warned me not to trip over her feet. With laughter, she responded, "Yes, I've got big feet!" I quickly responded, "I wear a size 12!" We're both tall, so I wasn't surprised when she said she wears an 11. I looked at Brad, Susan, and Linda, pointed from my feet to the top of my head, laughed, and asked, "Can you imagine all of this on little feet?"

God created me with big feet to support my body. He knew He needed to! We laughed at how awkward Susan and I would look if we wore size 6 or 7 shoes. And, more significantly, we'd likely fall over. We need a firm foundation to support our bodies.

We often think about God being our 'rock.' I hope He is that for you![1]

Your character instruction needs another foundation. Beliefs! As I've written, your beliefs, and your children's, cause behavior. Allow me to share several categories of beliefs you'll want to think about with yourself and your children in mind.

WHAT SHOULD CHILDREN BELIEVE ABOUT GOD AND HIS WORD?

Beliefs about God and His Word are foundational to all of life. This is especially true for adopting and maintaining a biblical worldview and living out biblical character. We don't want children just to be moral or good. We want them to have all that a biblical character offers them: strength from God, motivation from Jesus Christ, the empowerment of the Holy Spirit, and so much more! These things stand out to me as significant and necessary beliefs if children are to develop and use a biblical character.

Maybe the statements below can serve as a partial summary. Would your children make these claims? If they don't, and you agree they're vital, what can you do to help them believe these truths? Prioritizing God and His ways and parenting intentionally will help your children be able to state truths like the following:

- I believe my faith must be in Christ. I want to please God! I don't want to place my faith in myself or anyone else. It's not that I have strong enough faith. It's that God is strong enough. Mom and Dad have taught me Hebrews 11:6—"And without faith it is impossible to please him, for whoever would draw near to God must believe that he exists and that he rewards those who seek him." (See also Proverbs 3:5–6, Mark 9:23, Luke 1:37, and Matthew 21:22.) I believe the Bible is a trustworthy source of authority for me. It contains the teachings of God and Christ and guides my life. My parents are teaching me why they think it's accurate, dependable, and relevant, and they're helping me understand it more and more.[2] I'm not scared anymore to admit when I don't understand something. Second Timothy 3:16–17 has helped me—"All Scripture is inspired by God and is useful to teach us what is true and to make us realize what is wrong in our lives. It corrects us when we are wrong and teaches us to do what is right. God uses it to prepare and equip his people to do every good work" (NLT). (See also Isaiah 40:8, John 17:17, and 2 Peter 1:20–23.)
- I believe God is who He says He is and is on my side. I want to believe, follow Him, and become like Christ. I'm learning a lot about His character and actions from Psalm 25 and other

passages. Some of my favorite verses are Psalm 46:1 ("God is our refuge and strength, an ever-present help in trouble"), 1 John 1:9 ("If we confess our sins, he is faithful and just to forgive us our sins and to cleanse us from all unrighteousness"), and Jeremiah 31:3 ("I have loved you with an everlasting love; therefore I have continued my faithfulness to you").

- I believe God has called me to live an abundant life! I love that Mom and Dad taught me this. God wants us to have a rich and full life. I'm so glad! I like telling my friends this. Some think Jesus died for them only so they go to heaven when they die. I'm glad we do, but we get to live for Jesus now. Living with His joy and purpose and God's strength and energy is how we say "thank you" for His sacrifice. John 10:10 is true—"The thief comes only to steal and kill and destroy. I came that they may have life and have it abundantly."

What other beliefs about God and His Word do you need to prioritize? Think about your children's current character, behavior, and questions. They will show you their needs.

WHAT DOES JESUS BELIEVE ABOUT CHILDREN?

When studying for my doctorate in educational psychology and reading, I was required to research and draw conclusions about what made teaching effective. I read the required books and resources I chose, including one about teaching in the 1800s. That, as well as the memories teaching my second-grade students, inspired me to go back further—to the teaching of Jesus Christ. Studying Scripture with this new purpose inspired my curiosity about beliefs causing behavior.

Why did Jesus do what He did and say what He said? His beliefs were different.

Obviously, Jesus did not come to earth to demonstrate effective teaching methods. But we'd be foolish not to consider the way He taught. He was and still is the best teacher! We're still living by what He taught. We'll look at His methods in the next chapter. For now, know they're founded on His beliefs.

Reading and reflecting on Jesus' interactions with children as recorded in the Gospels especially inspired me. I've always thought and taught that our attitudes toward learners, whether they be your children or students in a classroom, are foundational to our success. These attitudes, reflected in our demeanor and interactions, come from our beliefs about them, ourselves, and the content we teach. Because Jesus' behaviors and statements were so different from others, it was obvious that His beliefs were different. Why did Jesus do what He did and say what He said? His beliefs were different.

When Jesus was here on earth, children were largely ignored. But not by Jesus. That's why Jesus' interactions with them would have been met with surprise and even anger from adults. Clearly,

He believed differently. I'll list some conclusions based on the following verses.[3]

Jesus' Interactions with Children

- "Then children were brought to him that he might lay his hands on them and pray. The disciples rebuked the people, but Jesus said, 'Let the little children come to me and do not hinder them, for to such belongs the kingdom of heaven.' And he laid his hands on them and went away." (Matt. 19:13–15)

- "And they were bringing children to him that he might touch them, and the disciples rebuked them. But when Jesus saw it, he was indignant and said to them, 'Let the children come to me; do not hinder them, for to such belongs the kingdom of God. Truly, I say to you, whoever does not receive the kingdom of God like a child shall not enter it.' And he took them in his arms and blessed them, laying his hands on them." (Mark 10:13–16)

- "Jesus called a little child to him and put the child among them. Then he said, 'I tell you the truth, unless you turn from your sins and become like little children, you will never get into the Kingdom of Heaven. So anyone who becomes as humble as this little child is the greatest in the Kingdom of Heaven. And anyone who welcomes a little child like this on my behalf is welcoming me. But if you cause one of these little ones who trusts in me to fall into sin, it would be better for you to have a large millstone tied around your neck and be drowned in the depths of the sea.'" (Matt. 18:2–6 NLT)

What do you see in these verses? Jesus slowed down and took time with children when others didn't. He was mad at the disciples for making it hard for people to come to Him with their children. He honored children's simple faith and thought so highly of them that He encouraged adults to become like them. He touched and blessed children. He equated receiving children in His name as receiving Him. He strongly rebuked adults who cause children who believe in Him to sin.

Jesus' Beliefs

What beliefs may have caused Jesus' choices? He thought children were worth blessing and taking time for. They were valuable and loved. They were acceptable, respected, understood, and their needs were more important than His own. He believed in them and was positive with them. Do you agree?

His beliefs caused His behavior, which caused the children's beliefs and behavior. But not only that. His beliefs influenced the adults who were watching and listening as well.

Picture the scene when the disciples asked Jesus who was the greatest in the kingdom of heaven. How might they have reacted when Jesus answered by having a child stand with Him? I picture them whispering among themselves, *Did He hear the question right?* They would have been shocked. And while the children would have felt honored, they would have also been confused, since being treated in this way was a new experience.

I remember the first time the Holy Spirit used this phrase in my life: "Let the little children come to me." When I taught second graders, I went outside with them during some recess breaks, sharing the recess-duty responsibility with my colleagues. Sometimes, as we were heading outside, I would try to convince the children that although I could see and talk with them, they couldn't see or talk with me. I remember saying, "Pretend I'm standing in a big, magic box."

Pushing children aside isn't how God would want us to behave.

Clearly, I thought I needed a break even while being on duty. Inevitably, while watching the students, I would hear the Spirit say, *Jesus took time for children, and He was tired and had a more critical agenda than you'll ever have.* God has often used this example from Jesus to set my priorities straight. His words and behavior caused children to know they mattered. It's how they knew they were significant and worth knowing. I wanted my students to know I believed these things, too, so I could encourage and influence them. Therefore, I would tear down the invisible box and interact with them.

Pushing children aside isn't how God would want us to behave.

What Jesus Wants Children to Believe About Themselves

Many years ago, when training Christian school teachers, I asked them to study the above passages and list what they believed Jesus wanted children to believe about themselves.[4] Their list is compelling! You could do the same exercise for yourself. Or list what *you* want your children to believe. Then ask yourself what beliefs you'll need to have for these beliefs to be their reality.

Here are teachers' answers, in the order they shared them:

Accepted	Important	Cared for	Treasured
Loved	Respected	Joyful	Trusted
Safe	Be themselves	Precious	Significant
Secure	Great potential	Listened to	Enjoyed
Comforted	Beautiful	Curious	Encouraged
Valuable	Worthy	Uninhibited	
Special	Happy	Blessed	

Celebrate Kids

Before founding my ministry, I had been a teacher of second graders, middle school coach, school board member, and professor. God used Deuteronomy 6:4–9 and the verses above to show me that I should quit my professorship, move across the country, and establish a ministry to help parents especially. I remember where I was when I knew deep down that I was to name my ministry Celebrate Kids. As I studied Jesus' interactions with children, prayed, and talked with friends, I saw that Jesus celebrated kids when others didn't. Thus, the name. Now all of us at the ministry pray that God will use us to help parents, grandparents, and educators celebrate kids for who they are and not just for what they do!

Aligning Beliefs with Scripture

Your beliefs about children influence *their* beliefs, which in turn cause their feelings, attitudes, and behavior, including character and obedience. Do you need to change any beliefs about your children? Would adopting some of Jesus' be fruitful? Do your children need new beliefs about themselves that they can develop because of yours? You can do this when you parent differently!

If children's beliefs about themselves don't align with Scripture, everything is more challenging. For example, if they don't think they matter, nothing matters. Character and obedience are irrelevant. Learning is optional. They won't be motivated to listen to you. They may increasingly doubt God's truth. Prioritize what you want them to believe about who they are and who they can be. Among other things, include statements about their learning abilities because, as we'll see later, they must believe they can learn.

> *If children don't think they matter, nothing matters.*

BELIEFS ABOUT PARENTS

What beliefs do you think children need to have about *you* so they'll listen, learn, and want to develop and use biblical character? They might believe, "My parents won't reject me when I mess up," "My parents understand how I feel," and "My parents will encourage and help me."[5]

If your relationship with your children is challenging right now, consider what beliefs would improve it. Don't think first about behaviors you need to change or you want children to exhibit. Think first about beliefs.

Because I was curious, I asked Facebook friends what they think their children need to believe about them. Fifty-one percent wrote that their children must know they, the parents, are trustworthy and honest. I was glad to see this. If you remember from chapter 4, security is the first core need that must be met.

I love what Laura wrote: "When it comes to discipline, no empty threats." And Camille wrote, "That you are their best safe person." That's smart because you should want your children to have many people they can turn to. Many moms wrote that they want their children to understand they want what's best for them and believe they're not looking out for their own selfish interests.

What beliefs would you prioritize? How will these show up in your behaviors? Which behaviors will indicate they believe what you want them to believe?

What Do You Need to Believe about Yourself?

You're the perfectly imperfect parent for your perfectly imperfect children, or they wouldn't be *your* children. God chose you to be a family and you're their best parent even on your worst day.[6] Remember this on tough and challenging days. God knew what He was doing when He made you a family—whether through birth, adoption, blended families, or fostering!

When asking my Facebook friends what they must believe about themselves, 35 percent mentioned this idea that God designed the family. Believing this affects your hope, patience, confidence, and more![7] No other belief came up as frequently.

In my survey, several friends listed this sentiment expressed by my friend Hannah: "I need to trust and believe that my value is not based on how well my kids turn out." Several, including Hannah, commented that they can't make their children behave and they can't fix everything. Parenting with grace and mercy as they rely on God was also mentioned. Yes, yes, and yes!

What do you need to believe about yourself? Your beliefs cause your behaviors and can influence your children's beliefs and behaviors. You matter!

BELIEFS ABOUT LEARNING

Children's beliefs about God, the Bible, you, and themselves are foundational to their joy, gratitude, self-efficacy, other character qualities, and . . . everything else! Let me also suggest that their beliefs about learning matter more than you might realize.

For you to influence your children, you need them to value learning. If they don't, all your efforts may be for naught. They may not listen, try new ideas, be humble or teachable, or be able to change culture. To take education seriously, children must believe learning at home, school, and church are essential. They also must think they're capable of learning. Of course, being incapable doesn't matter if they don't care about learning, wisdom, and growth. Writing about this is beyond the scope of this book, so I encourage you to read my book *8 Great Smarts*.

> *To take education seriously, children must believe they're capable of learning.*

The Master Learning Principles: What the Bible Says

Parent differently so children develop the master learning principles revealed in Scripture. This means you must be a master learner too.

How many of the biblical beliefs about learning listed below are true for your children? What's the evidence? If you need them to change their beliefs, observe and possibly change your beliefs and behavior. Remember, they learn from who you are and what you do.

- Learners respect God. "The fear of the LORD is the beginning of knowledge; fools despise wisdom and instruction" (Prov. 1:7). (See also Prov. 9:10, 14:26–27.)

- Learners pray for wisdom. "If you need wisdom, ask our generous God, and he will give it to you. He will not rebuke you for asking" (James 1:5 NLT). (See also 2 Chron. 1:10–12.)

- Learners value learning, wisdom, and instruction, especially God's wisdom. "Keep hold of instruction; do not let go; guard her, for she is your life" (Prov. 4:13). (See also Prov. 3:21; 4:7–8; 8:10–11; 9:9.)

- Learners value remembering. "My son, do not forget my teaching, but let your heart keep my commandments, for length of days and years of life and peace they will add to you" (Prov. 3:1–2). (See also Prov. 4:5; 1 Chron. 16:12.)

- Learners pay attention to gain understanding. "My children, listen when your father corrects you. Pay attention and learn good judgment" (Prov. 4:1 NLT). (See also Prov. 4:6, 20; 12:15.)

- Learners use new ideas. "What you have learned and received and heard and seen in me—practice these things, and the God of peace will be with you" (Philip. 4:9). (See also Matt. 7:24–27; John 13:1–17; James 1:22–25.) Remember what we covered in chapter 1. We want children to *use* character and not just *have* character.

- Learners praise God for wisdom. I love Daniel's example! "Blessed be the name of God forever and ever, to whom belong wisdom and might. . . . He gives wisdom to the wise and knowledge to those who have understanding; he reveals deep and hidden things; he knows what is in the darkness, and the light dwells with him. To you, O God of my fathers, I give thanks and praise, for you have given me wisdom and might" (Dan. 2:20–23). (See also Col. 3:16–17.)

BELIEFS ABOUT CHANGE

Before I wrap up this chapter, let me briefly address the topic of change. If you want to parent differently, what I share here matters. Why? If your children think change is always difficult or that it isn't possible, they'll resist your input.

Ephesians 4:22–24 makes it clear that change is a process that requires taking off the old unwanted belief and behavior and putting on the new. This is why I list some of the opposite, negative qualities for each of the forty-eight positive traits I include in the appendix.

When you read below about the qualities I recommend you prioritize, think about opposing beliefs, attitudes, and behaviors that get in the way. Just discussing the quality you want your children to own without addressing the negatives they need to disown will be less effective. Talk about both. And remember that because beliefs cause behavior, also address suspected beliefs leading to negative choices. I'll address this more in the next chapter, but I want you to think about this now.[8]

BELIEFS ABOUT CHARACTER

All of this can be true, but if children don't care about character and the resulting obedience, you're still stuck. Children may be resistant, disrespectful, immature, and dependent on you.

Remember what we covered in chapter 1—"When children realize they *can* be good, they may *want* to be good." These significant beliefs will make parenting easier. In addition, everything can improve when your children believe in their value, understand the purposes of traits, the beauty of having a positive reputation, and the importance of being obedient for God's glory and their good (and not just for yours).

These understandings can cause children to be more teachable, open to correction, and motivated to use the traits to change culture. Therefore, I'll share explanations about each quality's value.[9] I encourage you to add your thoughts about each, considering your family's values, children's needs, and what you've observed lately about their attitudes and behaviors. Remember their needs when you discern why these qualities are relevant.

Gratitude: Grateful children are more aware of what they have than what they do not have. They express thanks for blessings, kindness, support, and more. This quality depends on and increases inner peace, contentment, joy, and optimism. Gratitude affects identity and purpose and causes faithfulness, generosity, purposeful living, and healthy relationships. That's a lot—it's been identified as a "parent virtue" that positively increases spiritual maturity.[10] A dynamic relationship with Jesus Christ establishes its consistency and vibrancy.

Gratitude has been identified as a "parent virtue" that positively increases spiritual maturity.

"Give thanks in all circumstances;
for this is the will of God in Christ Jesus for you."
1 Thessalonians 5:18

Joy: Joyful children have a strong, positive sense of delight. They enjoy celebrating life. This quality depends on forgiveness, peace, contentment, gratitude, and life purpose. It affects identity and belonging. Joy is especially relevant to developing patience, kindness, other-centeredness, optimism, and energy. A dynamic relationship with Jesus Christ establishes consistency and vibrancy and allows them to rejoice in all circumstances.

". . . for the joy of the LORD is your strength."
Nehemiah 8:10

Self-Efficacy: Children with the quality of self-efficacy know they can be effective, and they accomplish their goals. They have initiative and are purposeful, optimistic, energetic, helpful, loving, and ready to serve. This quality is primarily related to purpose and competence.

"Commit your work to the LORD,
and your plans will be established."
Proverbs 16:3

Self-Respect: Children with self-respect have proper esteem for who they are. This quality motivates children to want all the other attributes and it helps them respond well to negativity. Self-respect is essential for security, purposeful living, good mental health, mature relationships, optimism, integrity, and service. It's the most critical quality related to children developing an inner moral code to do or say what's right, often despite external consequences and never merely because of them. This internal, personal, moral voice means their conscience isn't available for sale to the highest bidder. They'll operate consistently. They know what's right and wrong and good and evil and don't quickly change their mind because of what someone else believes. They will choose to be good over looking good.

"I praise you, for I am fearfully and wonderfully made.
Wonderful are your works; my soul knows it very well."
Psalm 139:14

Self-Control: Children with self-control can control their feelings and actions, even when they're tempted. This quality empowers children to use other attributes well and to behave in an orderly manner. Self-control is beneficial, especially for security and identity. They'll be productive, patient, humble, and less frustrated with themselves. They have impulse control and base their choices on their values, not their circumstances.

> "A person without self-control is like
> a city with broken-down walls."
> Proverbs 25:28 NLT

Other-Centeredness (Respect for Others): Children who are other-centered respect others and put them and their needs above their own. This quality motivates children to use qualities to benefit others, which is their purpose. It will be the root of healthy belonging and relationships. They'll be more thoughtful, considerate, compassionate, cooperative, and unselfish.

> "Do nothing from selfish ambition or conceit,
> but in humility count others more significant than yourselves."
> Philippians 2:3

Humility: Humble children are not arrogant and do not think they're better than others. This quality motivates children to be teachable, interested, willing to work, and submissive. They understand they're not perfect, can't operate only on their strength, and need all the qualities, including being patient, determined, forgiving, remorseful, and at peace.

> "Haughtiness goes before destruction;
> humility precedes honor."
> Proverbs 18:12 NLT

Resilient: Resilient children recover readily from disappointment, failure, defeat, adversity, and trauma. They willingly try new things. This quality leads to growth, creative problem-solving, confidence, and more. It prevents a victim mentality and mental health struggles.[11]

> "Dear brothers and sisters, when troubles of any kind come your
> way, consider it an opportunity for great joy. For you know that
> when your faith is tested, your endurance has a chance to grow.
> So let it grow, for when your endurance is fully developed,
> you will be perfect and complete, needing nothing."
> James 1:2–4 NLT

Discernment: Discerning children are alert and use appropriate standards to recognize and classify what's true, good, healthy, etc. This quality results in mature security, identity, and belonging.

These children have integrity and healthy relationships and are aware, fair, focused, forgiving, and remorseful.

"All things are lawful, but not all things are helpful.
All things are lawful, but not all things build up."
1 Corinthians 10:23

Brave: Courageous children confidently face obstacles and expect the best outcome. This quality allows children to do what's right even when the burden is heavy. They are secure and will stand up for themselves and others. They're also willing to take risks and try new things. This quality is vital for identity and purpose and relies on them taking the initiative, caring, and being compassionate, discerning, and confident.

"Have I not commanded you? Be strong and courageous.
Do not be frightened,and do not be dismayed, for the LORD
your God is with you wherever you go."
Joshua 1:9

Effort: Children who use effort work hard. With positive experiences, hard work can lead to diligence (consistent effort over time) and perseverance (effort despite difficulties). This quality facilitates humility, success, growth, teachability, maturity, and productivity.

"In all toil there is profit,
but mere talk tends only to poverty."
Proverbs 14:23

Compassion: Compassionate children feel someone's pain and want to help. This quality positively affects relationships, leads to service, and motivates kindness, gentleness, and helpfulness. It motivates them to be other-centered and it increases the health of belonging and purpose.

"Put on then, as God's chosen ones, holy and
beloved, compassionate hearts, kindness, humility,
meekness, and patience."
Colossians 3:12

Generous: Generous children give more of their time, re-sources, and talents than is usual or expected. When choosing these essential qualities, I didn't initially include generosity. I added it when I saw its relationship to the core needs, purposeful living, other-centeredness, and healthy decision-making. These children are not focused on themselves, but are willing to sacrifice to bless and serve others and are grateful, faithful, content, aware, joyful, friendly, kind, confident, optimistic, and healthy.

"The generous will prosper;
those who refresh others will themselves be refreshed."
Proverbs 11:25 NLT

QUESTIONS TO CONSIDER

1. While reading this chapter, have you thought about some of your negative behaviors and their associated beliefs? What are some opposite beliefs you need to adopt to change behaviors? What will help you make the changes permanent?

2. In your own words, how can you teach your children that beliefs cause behaviors?

3. If I asked your children what they believe about you, how do you predict they'd answer? What are new beliefs you'd love them to have about you?

4. Which of the thirteen character qualities will you prioritize for each of your children? Why? What's a first step you can take to begin the teaching process?

"A disciple is not above his teacher, but everyone
when he is fully trained will be like his teacher."
Luke 6:40

What STRATEGIES Can You Use for Teaching CHARACTER? (Part One)

I didn't want to write a book just about "good character" or "morality." Because of my biblical worldview and call to serve Christian parents, biblical character matters more to me. Maybe you have already experienced benefits of prioritizing this. Has your character matured? And has parenting gotten easier and your home calmer as your children have become more mature and obedient?

God wants us to prioritize our character. It's why He looks at the heart, as we read in 1 Samuel 16:7—"But the LORD said to Samuel, 'Don't judge by his appearance or height, for I have rejected him. The LORD doesn't see things the way you see them. People judge by outward appearance, but the LORD looks at the heart'" (NLT). But He doesn't just look at our heart; He tests the heart: "The crucible is for silver, and the furnace is for gold, and the LORD tests hearts" (Prov. 17:3).

Psalm 139 ends with these verses: "Search me, O God, and know my heart! Try me and know my thoughts! And see if there be any grievous way in me, and lead me in the way everlasting!" Sometimes when teaching and wanting to make certain points, I read it out loud and change the ending: "Search me, O God, and know my heart! Try me and know my thoughts! And see if there be any grievous way in me, and *punish me accordingly!*" Oh, how I praise God that this isn't true! He searches our hearts so He can lead us to truth. The more you and your children know God, the

The more you and your children know God, the less fearful you'll all be about the reality that He searches and tests our hearts.

less fearful you'll all be about the reality that He searches and tests our hearts. We can trust Him to lead us well!

I'm grateful the Holy Spirit is active in the life of believers. Without Him, I know I wouldn't be who I am. Perhaps you can also say this about your life. We don't have to depend on ourselves! He is the One who transforms hearts and helps us become more like Jesus. John 14:26 makes it clear: "But the Helper, the Holy Spirit, whom the Father will send in my name, he will teach you all things and bring to your remembrance all that I have said to you."

You're not in this alone. You get to partner with God in this vital parenting work! You've already read and considered many ideas. The ideas in this chapter and the next for teaching character qualities will further encourage you.

DEPEND ON GOD

If you remember what I wrote in chapter 3 about the blessings of children being God-centered, you'll want to take Him seriously when working to improve children's character. For your children to develop and use biblical character, they need to believe in God and trust Christ as their Savior. As a result, they'll have His strength and insight and the gift and leading of the Holy Spirit. If children don't yet know Jesus, teach all you can about Him. Prioritize their spiritual development and growth in their biblical worldview. You want them saved! Celebrate progress and growth in their understandings, commitment, and love.

Introduce them to Christian relational activities—prayer, reading and studying Scripture, church involvement, worship, fellowship, service, family and personal devotions, journaling and writing out Scripture, fellowship, fasting, and celebrations like communion and baptism. Teach them age-appropriate understandings of why and how we do each of these. Defining each with your children can be an interesting educational and spiritual exercise. For example, in my church, we define prayer as an ongoing

In my church, we define prayer as an ongoing conversation with our best friend while we're on a long journey.

conversation with our best friend while we're on a long journey.[1]

Do these activities with your children, encourage *them* to lead you in them, and do them independently. Teach them how to recognize and respond to the Holy Spirit's leading. You can also learn about missionaries together. They're often beautiful examples of maturity, commitment, call, service, and sacrifice.[2] Trips to museums can also increase children's curiosity and spark meaningful conversations. What else can you think of?

REMEMBER IT'S A PROCESS

Remember that teaching character is a process. You won't have a linear one-and-done discussion and see major changes in your children. Rather, you'll have ongoing conversations, circle back to ideas to correct false thinking, and add details as necessary. If you forget this, you can easily become overwhelmed and frustrated.

You may start with rote teaching of definitions, benefits, and how-to steps and have children repeat your exact words. Then you can move on to having them put things into their own words. They can act out what qualities would look and feel like. They can talk about the benefits of each quality. They can talk with you about successes and awkward moments they had when using the qualities. To be successful, you'll teach a lot. New experiences and relationships will require updated explanations. Children will make mistakes and need opportunities to try again. The ideas below will help you as I pray the ideas above will. If you parent differently, you won't lose heart or give up.

DON'T OVERPROTECT YOUR CHILDREN

I want to comment briefly on the value of trials and struggles. They're part of the process God uses to teach character. Experiencing the value and victory of recovery is so important to me that I included resiliency in my top thirteen qualities. Disappointments and challenges are a part of life! Recovering well increases children's confidence, hope, optimism, joy, gratitude, self-efficacy, and nearly everything else! Children who don't learn how to succeed during and after difficulties may struggle for much of life.

Romans 5:3–4 teaches us that "suffering produces endurance, and endurance produces character, and character produces hope." If you look back on your life experiences, you'll undoubtedly conclude that your character matured and your faith and hope grew as you faced and walked through challenging times. Therefore, don't overprotect your children. Support them during times of difficulty, teach them how to be alert to life's pitfalls, but don't regularly step in to save them from challenges. They will discover mature character from living through tough times.

DETERMINE WHY CHILDREN DO WHAT THEY DO

What children believe about themselves, you, God, learning, character, and more makes all the difference. So do your beliefs. Remember, identity controls behavior and identity is shaped by beliefs. Beliefs must change for behaviors to change. But there are other reasons children do what they do. Let's think about those too.

Prioritize Discovering and Changing Children's Beliefs

Help your children discern why they do what they do. Why are they kind sometimes and unkind at other times? Why is generosity hard for them? Why do they get outraged when someone isn't fair? What experiences have formed their beliefs?

Children often don't know why they do what they do.

Children often don't know why they do what they do. Uncovering their beliefs so you can reinforce them or change them requires you to observe. Look for inconsistencies, changes in attitudes, and behaviors like secrecy that will suggest why they do what they do.

Watch for their reactions as you make statements to predict what might be going on. Ask questions and watch eye contact and body language that sometimes shows you what's true. Listen for what they don't say. This can also help you predict what they're thinking about.

Determine Other Reasons Children Make Unwise Choices

If you can determine why children do what they do, your interventions will be more successful. Observe with your eyes and ears. Look for patterns. Know your children! Children aren't impatient, prideful, or argumentative every day.

Keeping a written record will help you discover triggers. For example, it may not take long to discover your son brags and competes with a brother only after not doing well on an assignment or during a game. He's insecure and disappointed and doesn't know how to handle it. Or, you may have a daughter who is occasionally impatient, agitated, and pessimistic, none of which are her typical behaviors. You notice this happens when her dad offers to help with math homework, but not during other times. You talk with him and the two of you discern how he can interact differently with her. You keep track of her character and see that she responds well to his changes.

Knowing children's triggers allows you to teach them to become aware so they can stop negative choices before they start. When children choose to behave immaturely and are disobedient, quickly write down the circumstances. To help you discover patterns, note what was going on, who was present, what time it was, and where you were. You can do this when you're home, in line at a store, on the way to or from practices, or visiting at your mom's. Some parents keep a running list on paper taped to an inside kitchen cupboard door. Others keep notes in their phone and compare those notes with their spouse.

If you start keeping track of children's outbursts and other choices that frustrate you, you'll likely discover they're often thirsty, hungry, tired, or bored. Start here—have them drink water before discussing their choices. They'll now listen better. You could also share a snack with them. If they realize they feel better, in the future, they may drink more water and ask for a snack without you intervening. Something this simple can prevent poor choices and disobedience. Of course, there may be health issues. Always be willing to consult with medical professionals.

If you believe fatigue is a factor, you now have evidence that you need to put them to bed earlier or add a nap or quiet time into the day. The consequence for their immature choices and misbehavior is rest. If boredom is a factor, teach them what they can do when bored. Together, make lists of fun and practical ideas and help them remember to look there when they're bored.

I'm grateful for all your efforts and your desire to parent differently. I'm sure you are, too! Yet, you know you're imperfect—perfectly imperfect! You may occasionally be a factor in your children's poor choices. Peers and others can also be a factor.[3] This is why teaching about friendship is important and discernment regarding people's motives is worth teaching.[4]

Perhaps your children haven't had enough instruction on the new quality you want them to use or enough experience with a new situation. Do they feel safe enough to ask you for help? If they think they'll just get yelled at, they may not.

Does your child feel safe enough to ask you for help?

Children may experience doubt and fear because of the tension they feel from something going on at home. Maybe you make comparisons, or they compare themselves to siblings on their own. If they consistently feel they can't measure up, they may not put forth their best effort. This is also true if they think perfectionism is the standard or your expectations are unrealistic. Disappointment, depression, and loneliness can cause children to choose character qualities you'd rather they not use.

What else do you think of? You may be inconsistent or not always follow through. There are many possibilities—which is a reason to keep a written record. You'll find that each child usually has a few triggers. You may also discover that certain negative qualities, like being uncooperative, inflexible, dishonest, and apathetic, are consistently caused by the same or similar issues. Learning what causes the problems gives you something to change that can, in turn, change your children's character.

MUCH IS CAUGHT *AND* TAUGHT

Parent educators often say, "More is caught than taught." I understand. Your example is powerful! I can't help but wonder, though, if more is caught than taught because not enough is taught. I pray you'll take both of your roles seriously. You can be both an example of biblical character and a teacher of biblical character. Dare I say you must be? Both functions allow you to equip your children to glorify God with their choices and change culture with their actions.

What does good role modeling involve? Work to use the top thirteen qualities, other qualities in the list of forty-eight, and still other traits that come to mind. Use the "one anothers," fruit of the Spirit, the Beatitudes, and attributes from Christ's life. Talk is cheap, but back your comments up with action and your children will more willingly listen. We all know that more fruit results when the walk and the talk match.

Strive for integrity, consistency, and compassion. These establish and maintain the essential core need of security. Quickly apologize when you should, ask for forgiveness when you sin against children, and promptly forgive them if they sin against you. And, let them know you have. Don't make them wonder if you've been full of mercy and grace for them. Then, work to not remind children of their sin just as God doesn't remind us of ours.[5] Promptly and humbly dealing with sin is essential for solid joy and gratitude.

But please understand that forcing children to forgive you doesn't work. You can tell them you hope they will, but forcing them to before they're ready can add another wound to your relationship. And, as I often teach, be careful of explaining yourself or defending yourself. This can make them feel guilty and responsible even if that's not your intent.

Explaining—and Showing

In your role modeling and teaching, stress purposes of the qualities. My explanations in the previous chapter can help. Also, use what you realize is true in your situations. Point out that you don't cooperate so others will. You cooperate because it's who you are. It's a value and part of your inner moral code. You don't act with kindness to get something you want, or only when others are kind. You're kind because it's who you are, not just what you do.

Demonstrate your peace, purposeful living, and joy. Connect with God's strength in you and passion for you so your children see it. Let them see you putting others first and being brave. Share times when resiliency was necessary, discernment saved you from significant trouble, and effort resulted in great victories.

Sometimes explain why you do what you do. Don't assume your children will always connect the dots and figure it out. They might not pay close enough attention. And, if you always explain, they'll develop negative attitudes about character and disrespect

149

you. Sometimes ask them why they think you do what you do. Affirm their insights when you can. Correct them when you should.

For instance, if you're busy, why would you make a meal for your neighbor or someone from church you don't know? If you just told your children there isn't enough money to buy them something they want, why do you contribute when a ministry invites you to? If you're an introvert, why would you host a church committee meeting in your home?

Let them see you putting others first.

As you model mature character and share about your life experiences, do your best not to be prideful. You're doing this to help your children, not to build up yourself. You don't want them to think they're competing with you. You don't want to contradict your teaching that we need to be at a place where we do what's right even when no one is looking. Stress the audience of one—God!

Bible Heroes as Role Models

Bible heroes can be your best role models. You can point out their character when you're doing family devotions or when your children tell you what they learned in a class or chapel, and you can create specific lessons to make valuable points. The men and women in Scripture are there on purpose. Learn alongside your children and benefit from them.

Jesus going to the cross for us and washing the feet of the

disciples, including Judas, the night before His crucifixion, are the best examples of humility you can find. Of course, finishing what He set out to do for us is an example of diligence, perseverance, and obedience. Paul comes to mind for persistence and resiliency. Daniel "resolved that he would noto defile himself" in Babylon, and this choice served Him well.[6] How could you use him as an example with your children? What character qualities are embedded in the example of Esther who "obeyed Mordecai just as when she was brought up by him"?[7]

Who can you think of for faith? Love? Joy? Gratitude? Self-control? Changing culture? Sometimes negative examples teach well. Who was lazy, self-absorbed, entitled, worried, scared, stingy, and selfish? These people can teach your children who not to be. You get the idea. For your children to have and use biblical character that changes culture, use Scripture and all the wisdom and examples we have there.

As you can see, effective role modeling involves talking and explaining. In the rest of this chapter and the next, I'll share more ideas for teaching.

COMMUNICATE IN HELPFUL WAYS

All of us at Celebrate Kids believe that the words we speak and the words we don't speak change lives.[8] Your words hold significant weight. They're such an essential key to effective parenting that I devoted three chapters to communication in *Start with the Heart*, two chapters about conversations in *Resilient Kids*, and instruction about effective communication in my other books. One of my most popular talks at conventions for homeschoolers is titled "Parenting Power Words." Allow me to make these communication recommendations here:

Use the Word "Choice"

You perhaps have noticed throughout the book that I've used the word "choice" frequently. It's one of your most powerful words. Using it helps you teach your children that all behavior starts with choice, and this includes character. Your children choose to be other-centered or self-centered, resilient or fragile, and grateful or entitled. The power of choice is one of the reasons you need to prioritize family values and worldview. When they're rooted in God, there's a better chance that your children will choose biblical character qualities.

You might sound like this: "Jessica, I'm proud of you for *choosing* to be gentle even though your brother was teasing you. That was kind of you." Or, "Brian, I'm sorry you *chose* to be disrespectful. That wasn't wise. We've talked with you before about considering your sister and her lack of confidence. What can you *choose* to do differently later today?"

Use the Phrases "You are Being . . ." and "You are Not Being . . ."

Another way to emphasize that character is always a choice is to use phrases that use the word "being." For example, "you are being joyful" differs from "you are joyful." Do you see the difference? These children could have been pessimistic, apathetic, disagreeable, or merely happy. But they chose *this time* to be joyful. It doesn't mean they'll choose joy the next day.

Using these words and phrases will remind you to teach children to be more aware of their circumstances so they can make wise choices. That's how you and I choose who to be. We discern who we need to be. Of course, I pray that many qualities become a genuine part of who we are and we don't waver, no matter the burden we may feel and who is there. This is what I eventually want for your children. I think you do too. You can parent differently and do this! Children can make mature choices and *be* who they need to be.

Use Specific Compliments

Be specific when you affirm your children. Especially when children are first learning a strategy, you'll want to compliment them often to reinforce their choices. Then, once habits are established, random compliments are most effective for motivating continual use.

Being specific allows your children to repeat the positive behaviors or attitudes you call out of them. For example, if you tell them they're "nice," there's no guarantee they'll understand what you're referring to and how to repeat it. "Nice" is a word we use for many generic qualities and outcomes. Instead, refer to the appendix often enough and remember the thirteen top qualities so you can use these specific words.

For example, rather than saying, "That was nice," work to say, "You agreed quickly and respected your aunt." I wrote "work to say" because initially it may take effort for you to observe your children's circumstances carefully enough that you can point out the specific traits they used. You may be in the habit of telling children they're "good." But tell them what was good about what they did. Were they polite, diligent, grateful, or peaceful?

Being specific is powerful because your children will want to use these qualities again since you pointed them out and were encouraged by them.[9]

Use Specific Corrections

The same thing holds true for corrections. Be specific and not general. If you tell your children you're unhappy with them, they won't be empowered to change. Or if you announce the rather typical, "I don't want any more of that attitude!" they may be frustrated and not encouraged. Why were you unhappy? What was wrong with their attitude or character? Were they prideful, indifferent, hard-hearted, unfriendly, or pessimistic?

Bravely pointing out children's negatives gives them hope that they can change. They now know what negative behavior to take off and can figure out what to put on. Or, better yet, in case they don't know, tell them what they did that caused you to label them as "prideful, indifferent, hard-hearted, unfriendly, or pessimistic." Tell them what to put on instead. "Next time, rather than being indifferent and not caring about your brother, I know you will care and be determined to make a difference. That would mean you will listen longer, offer real help, and not be judgmental."[10]

> *Pointing out children's negatives gives them hope that they can change.*

USE CONSEQUENCES

As powerfully crucial as words are, you won't be able to only talk to children and correct them when you're disappointed by their character choices. Sometimes they will need to experience consequences for their choices.[11]

Natural Consequences

When children make wise and unwise character choices, they will experience natural consequences if you don't get in the way. They earn these and you have nothing to do with it. For example, if they gossip, friends may stop sharing vulnerable information with them for a while and they'll feel left out. Help them see that their friends are being silent as a direct consequence of their choice to gossip. Encourage them not to gossip and prove again that they're trustworthy.

If you discover they lied, they earn the natural consequence of you asking their piano teacher, soccer coach, or the relevant people if they're telling the truth. When your children complain, remind them that they *chose* your behavior because of how they behaved. After many positive reports, affirm your children's growing honesty, stay alert, and check on them randomly and occasionally.

When children choose to be responsible, you'll trust them with more independence. When they choose to submit, they'll be at peace and your relationship will be easy. When they choose to study and ask for help if they're confused, they'll do better on an assessment. Natural consequences are powerful teaching tools. Stay out of the way and ensure your children connect the dots to understand how these consequences work.

Logical Consequences

Logical consequences are also compelling. Like natural consequences, they're directly related to your children's choices, but these are thought of and implemented by you. For example, if children are caught gaming in their rooms instead of studying, either remove all devices from their rooms or require that they do their homework in the living room or den with you. These options fit the crime.

If children are entitled and prideful about all they have, you might make the decision that they choose ten toys or items of clothing to give away. They may not like this, but it's a logical consequence to curb pride. This can also work if they don't take care of their clothes, toys, devices, etc. Tell them it's obvious they have too much to take care of, so they need to give some of it away. Or, you will only buy them something new once they prove they can take care of what they own. Have them work with you to choose who to give the things to.

Pay attention and see what natural consequences you need to make space for and what logical consequences you can implement before you think about what punishments might work. This helps children learn independence. No one punishes you and me. We experience consequences for our wise and unwise choices. Your children will benefit from learning from those consequences.

QUESTIONS TO CONSIDER

1. What are your attitudes toward some of the Christian relational activities? Do you need more positive experiences so you can embrace them more fully? Who could you talk with and what could you do? How will you benefit?

2. In your own words, tell someone how looking for patterns in children's choices and character can benefit them and you. Choose an issue for one or two children and commit to uncovering patterns. When you find them, make decisions about what to do next. You could talk with your children, implement consequences, reteach, and more.

3. Start using the word "choice" or the phrases "you are being" and "you are not being" when talking with your children about their actions. Pay attention to how they make you feel and how your children respond. Make adjustments and keep up the excellent work.

4. Are there Bible heroes you can talk about and teach about as a family to bring up essential character qualities? Who? When and how will you do this?

"Let the wise hear and increase in learning,
and the one who understands obtain guidance."
Proverbs 1:5

What STRATEGIES Can You Use for Teaching CHARACTER? (Part Two)

I hope you've been encouraged to see there's much you can do to help your children learn and use character qualities. Let's continue with more ideas.

HAVE MEANINGFUL AND FOCUSED CONVERSATIONS

Although there will be times you will need to teach character qualities directly, informal conversations can also be compelling. Your children are reminded you care, and they learn what you're interested in. You also have opportunities to share your heart, inspiring them to share theirs. Conversations may be especially relevant for influencing and changing children's beliefs.

As your children talk about life and their day, they may not realize the value of what they share with you and what you're listening for. Therefore, they may be transparent, vulnerable, and honest. Listen for examples of their character and obedience. Make relevant comments and ask leading questions so you can talk about their beliefs and not just their actions. Through your conversations they'll learn that beliefs cause behavior.

Of course, you'll also want to share your beliefs. Talk about how self-efficacy makes you feel and why you choose it. Share about the beauty of glorifying God through your choices and their outcomes. Don't just share about what you do during the day, but why you do it. Did you help others and influence culture? How did you decide what to do? Point out how your character allows you to speak life and light into brokenness.

When you can, point out inconsistencies in your children's choices and behavior. Help them become more self-aware of what they do and why. When they're inconsistent, they're not using their inner moral code or haven't yet established one. Inconsistencies are built-in opportunities to teach and reteach character. Use teachable moments during your conversations and direct teaching later to point out what they did. Try to determine their motivation so you know what beliefs to address later.

Sometimes children will talk more when siblings aren't present. They also might prefer to open up to one parent at a time. Of course, if you're married, it's important to ensure both of you know what's going on. If you've been divorced and other parents are involved, ideally you all share with each other so goals for behavior are consistent and you treat children consistently. When that's not possible, do your best to explain the differences and treat your children consistently when they're with you. That's what you're responsible for.

I make many other suggestions in two chapters in *Resilient Kids* that will help you and your children relate well during conversations.[1] For example, talking in the dark works well; boys usually share more when they're busy; and when you need more information, there are better ways to get it than by interrogating them. Please check out this valuable resource.

TEACH LIKE A REPORTER THINKS

I sometimes say that we skill and drill the 1, 2, 3s and ABCs, but expect immediate compliance when urging our children to obey or respect boundaries. Yet Christlike character and obedience are more challenging to learn. Just like we break down reading and math into bite-size pieces that can be taught and absorbed, we must do the same with character.

When reporting on a story, reporters share details about *what* happened; *how, why, when,* and *where* it happened; and *who* was involved. Share these details when you initially teach the qualities. Reinforce and change them as children age and you expect them to use qualities more independently and broadly. For example, is it okay or not if they're generous only when they have a lot (sharing toys, for instance) and know the people, or do you expect them to be generous in all circumstances?

Or you may teach that honesty, respect, and caring are always expected and should not be controlled by who they're with, where they are, or the time. In other cases, you may expect children to start by using some qualities only with family and friends. Then the "who" may change to include acquaintances and strangers. For example, depending on your values and situations, being hospitable, decisive, and confident come to mind.

You can think this through for the other reporter details too. You may sometimes define the qualities, the *what*, differently because of ages and abilities. For example, what does other-centeredness look like for your child on the autism spectrum and your child without this diagnosis? What about the *why* and *how*? You may need to provide different explanations of why qualities are valuable because of a situation one of your children was involved in. Children's motivation and the way they learn best will influence the way you teach them how to do it. What about the *when* and *where* details? Do they sometimes change depending on your children's ages and their circumstances? Do you always want them to be careful, resourceful, and brave? Tell them that.

TEACH WITH THESE QUESTIONS IN MIND

I've used these questions to plan my teaching ever since I designed them as study strategies and taught them to my university students. (As I've mentioned, Jesus' teaching methods inspired me.) I used these when writing this book because I've had you in mind. Keep them in mind when you teach, reteach, and talk about character, themselves, you, and God.

What?—What do I want them to know? Believe? Do? Feel? Think?

So what?—What difference can it make?

Now what?—What are they going to do? Who are they going to be?

For example:

- What do I want my children to know about biblical character? Are there certain things I want them to believe, do, feel, and think?

I want them to *know* biblical character honors God and is a part of our family values. I want them to *believe* they can grow in maturity and that using the qualities consistently and automatically will get easier. I want them to *feel* supported as I look for their growth and point it out even as I reteach when needed. I want them to *think* optimistically about their attempts.

- So what? What difference can it make?

I will be less frustrated and more optimistic and positive toward my children. Therefore, they will be open to sharing their questions and spending time with me. My children will become more like Christ and honor God and me with their decisions. Our relationship will be even more positive than it has been.

- Now what? What are they going to do?

My children will keep growing in their ability to relate to people using biblical character. They will develop an inner moral code to do what's right even when the burden is heavy and I'm not watching.

- Now what? Who are they going to be?

My children will increasingly become more like Jesus Christ, and be happy to be associated with our family, surrounded by good people, and content, purposeful, and productive.

Relax! You only have to think or type up detailed thoughts like these if you want to. Speaking from experience, the thinking process will help you tremendously. It's easy to get distracted, but thinking of the what, so what, and now what can help you focus on primary goals and expectations. If you do this for one or two qualities you want to emphasize, you'll find great joy in the strategic thinking and then the success.

TEACH CONNECTED QUALITIES

As I've pointed out, character qualities don't work alone. Forgiveness requires other-centeredness and humility. Patience requires being hopeful and compassionate. You might think of other connections—there are plenty! If you want children to improve their consistent use of a quality, think about a second one to talk about and teach simultaneously. Your children may be more successful.

Character qualities don't work alone.

When your children don't choose to use a character quality they need, don't focus solely on it. Instead, observe and predict other qualities that are essential in this situation and talk about those. Also, is there a belief about God, you, themselves, learning, character, or something else they need in this situation? Is there another reason they're not being obedient? Pray for them, wait for teachable moments, and set up opportunities to teach and discuss what they need.

For example, children may be irritable and not agreeable. Maybe they're also tired, jealous, and confused. Talking about these might prove more beneficial than complaining about how irritable they are. Here's another example. Maybe children weren't self-controlled and they spilled something or yelled at someone. Perhaps they were also fearful, stressed, and embarrassed because they were caught cheating. These don't excuse their lack of self-control, but they can make it understandable and it will change your conversation and maybe the consequences you choose.

TEACH CHARACTER WITH DECISION-MAKING

Character affects so much. (I wonder if you can think of anything unaffected by character and character qualities. This question might be profitable to discuss with your children.) Character leads to choices—and choices have consequences.

Modeling and teaching how character influences decision-making will be a good use of your time. Every choice is a decision, so become alert to your children's choices and look for what traits they're using. Depending on what you notice, teachable moments may not be enough. Create and teach lessons structured with the reporter questions and my suggested questions above.

For example, how would self-centeredness influence decision-making? Maybe these children always choose the biggest cookie, make noise even though you or a sibling are trying to concentrate, and don't participate in a youth group service project because it doesn't interest them. How would fear show up? Maybe fearful children never volunteer to go first during activities, avoid visitors rather than welcome them, and blame others rather than owning responsibility for something that is their fault.

Of course, positive character choices affect children as well. For example, hopeful children willingly ask for help, volunteer even with no experience, and don't whine and complain as much as others. Compassionate children may choose to talk with people when they volunteer with you at the homeless shelter, ask you to pray about something that troubles them, and comfort sensitive children who are overwhelmed in a large group.

To increase their motivation and teachability, point out how children's character choices make them fulfilled or miserable. Notice that some of my examples are in the context of service. Serving others is another helpful way to increase motivation and help children see the impact of their character. Often they're more willing to be good when they're serving. This is what purpose does—it increases competence. (See more about decision-making and competence in *Five to Thrive*.²)

TEACH CHARACTER—STUDY JESUS' METHODS

In chapter 6, I wrote that studying the teaching ministry of Christ greatly affected me. He was and still is the best teacher! I want you to use some of His methods when teaching character qualities. We obviously can't be like Christ in terms of His deity, but Christ should be our model and source of strength in every other sense, including our teaching.

Jesus was frequently addressed as Teacher, and He referred to Himself as Teacher: "You call me Teacher and Lord, and you are right, for so I am" (John 13:13). Of course, more importantly, He

Always study your children. is Lord, Savior, Redeemer, and more.

Allow me to share just four of the methods that contributed to Christ's teaching excellence. If you want to, study this on your own. When you read the Gospels, what other methods, beliefs, or attitudes do you notice? What other verses could you list to support my conclusions?

For example:

- Jesus knew His "students."[3] Always study your children. What is their identity, and what are their needs, sin temptations, troublesome friendships, and goals? You're not teaching character to the masses. You're teaching it to *your* children. Individualize your choices and instruction!

- Jesus knew and used God's Word.[4] He was the Word and He used the Word when battling Satan. He used His education and His roots to fight. If Jesus used the Word, how much more important is it for us to do so? Use it accurately and sensitively. As children tell me, don't hit them over the head with it. Observe your children's attitudes.

- Jesus stayed focused and completed the work His Father gave Him to do.[5] I'm so grateful Jesus didn't get distracted, lose hope, or give up! He went all the way to the cross for us. I pray you stay focused on parenting strong and long. Keep the big picture in mind so tough days don't derail you.

- Jesus evaluated the effect of His teaching and retaught many times. For example, He returned to unrepentant cities and explained things more than once to His disciples.[6] I worded this intentionally. Evaluating your effect on your children is different from evaluating them. This approach will help you take appropriate responsibility for any part of a problem that might be yours, help children trust you, and improve attitudes! For example, when I taught, if the majority of my students struggled with an assignment, I didn't record those grades. Clearly, I hadn't taught well or explained something well. I owned it. You might sometimes admit that your impatience caused your children's. Or your lack of preparation stressed your children and caused their irritability. These realizations should cause you to react differently to their misbehavior.

TEACH CHARACTER—EIGHT WAYS TO BE SMART

When you teach your children according to the eight ways they're smart, they'll learn character better. They'll also be more successful using what they learned. If you have read my book 8 *Great Smarts*, you have possibly identified your children's smart strengths.[7] If that's the case, you can teach to their top one or two smarts. You can reteach to one of their strengths when they don't do well. If you don't know how your children are smart, my book can help you. And, if you simply teach to more than one part of the brain, your children will benefit. We tend to do most of our teaching by talking and asking questions. These are appropriate strategies, but they leave out much of the brain's thinking power and how some of your children think best. For example:

- Word smart—Use descriptive words, define words, allow children to talk and not just listen, have them write about the qualities and their behavior, and give them chances to persuade you respectfully. Explain and identify.

- Logic smart—Use questions and answers, record data about children's choices and behavior, and point out cause-effect relationships, comparisons and contrasts, and helpful sequences and steps to help them successfully use the qualities. Analyze and predict.

- Picture smart—Have children draw pictures of themselves being obedient, close their eyes and picture themselves making good character choices, and find examples related to something you're teaching in print and on billboards, TV shows, and advertising. Illustrate and describe.

- Music smart—Use music in the background to calm children, have them make up jingles and songs to help them remember how they want to behave, and read biographies of musicians they admire and look for examples of qualities like teachability, effort, and joy. Listen and classify.

- Body smart—Have children create skits so they can act out proper behavior in different situations, practice mature character like walking slowly to respect a grandmother, read biographies of athletes they respect, and teach them responses like doing "thumbs down" when they're confused or overwhelmed and need your help. Show and demonstrate.

- Nature smart—Spend time outside to relax children, talk outside because they may concentrate better, and point out patterns in their choices and behavior. Categorize and diagram.

- People smart—Discuss ideas, collaborate, and interact with children. Use interview formats and encourage them to work on related projects with siblings. Discuss and evaluate.

- Self smart—Give children time to think deeply, quietly, and alone. Encourage them to set goals and evaluate how they do in meeting them. Have them journal or keep logs of their character choices and behavior. Ponder and decide.

TEACH CHARACTER—THREE WAYS TO REMEMBER

God also generously designed children with three modalities, or memory channels, to use when wanting to remember things.[8] (You have all three also, just as you have all eight smarts.) Children can use these modalities to remember your instructions, how to behave, what to say, and more. They may have a strength, although that can change with age, so pay attention to what works so you can advise them. For example:

- Auditory modality—These children remember best what they hear and especially what they hear themselves say. Encourage them to talk to themselves and to others quietly. Don't make them listen too long without having the opportunity to speak.
- Visual modality—These children remember best the things they see. You can change your facial expressions when teaching qualities and act out behaviors for them to watch. Write out key words and instructions and have them study those.
- Kinesthetic modality—These children remember best the things they do. Let them act out the differences between patience and impatience, respect and disrespect. Encourage them to be physically active in mature ways.

AND NOW . . .

You persevered and finished! I sincerely pray you found hope in these pages for whatever situations motivated you to read my book. Perhaps you've chosen relevant Scripture to become more familiar with and to teach your children. Maybe Bible heroes or missionary stories are now a regular part of your routine. Hopefully some teaching ideas also stood out to you as worth trying and you've already been successful. I know I included a lot, so I hope you're planning to go back through these pages with specific goals in mind.

Maybe gathering as a family to decide which character qualities to start with would be another smart thing to do. Getting your children's buy-in from the very beginning will help. Remember my friend Kayla, who knows doing the next good thing is wise? She needed to take all six children (eight and under!) to her youngest son's doctor's appointment. Normally she wouldn't take them all. To prepare them, she read them our friend's book, *The Grumbles*, the night before.[9] They talked about the heart attitude they would all need to have. It worked! When she told me about it, she said, "The kids did incredible at the hospital. It couldn't have gone better!" Many children want to please their parents. They need to know how. Remember that.

QUESTIONS TO CONSIDER

1. What's your biggest frustration regarding conversations with your children? Can you talk with them about how to improve these and why? How could you create an opportunity to share new ideas?

2. Choose a character quality your entire family would benefit from improving. On your own or with your children, to plan effective teaching, write out answers to the reporter questions or the "what, so what, now what" questions.

3. What service project could you and your children participate in so they gain new understandings of the value of character?
4. What other qualities of Jesus' teaching excellence can you discover by reading some of the sections in the Gospels where He taught? How can you use what you learn?

"Show yourself in all respects to be a model of good works, and in your teaching show integrity, dignity, and sound speech that cannot be condemned, so that an opponent may be put to shame, having nothing evil to say about us."
Titus 2:7–8

APPENDIX

48 HEALTHY Qualities and Their OPPOSITES

Healthy Quality	Some Opposite, Unhealthy Qualities
Agreeable	Disagreeable, incompatible, mean
Brave	Afraid, fearful, timid, cowardly
Careful	Inattentive, careless, negligent, unaware
Caring	Uncaring, aloof, unfeeling, unfriendly
Compassionate	Unsympathetic, cold, unkind, uninterested
Confident	Apprehensive, doubtful, indefinite, uncertain, arrogant
Consistent	Inconsistent, unsteady, erratic
Cooperative	Uncooperative, divided, stubborn, self-centered
Decisive	Indecisive, inconclusive, indefinite, argumentative
Determined	Undetermined, apathetic, weak, indifferent
Diligent	Uninterested, lazy, inactive, careless, inattentive
Discerning	Undiscerning, unaware, negligent, undiscriminating
Effort	Lazy, idle, passive, unteachable
Fair	Unfair, biased, dishonest, prejudiced

Healthy Quality	Some Opposite, Unhealthy Qualities
Faithful	Faithless, careless, disloyal, unreliable
Flexibility	Inflexible, resistant, closed, stubborn
Forgiving	Hard-hearted, indifferent, unfeeling, judgmental
Generous	Greedy, selfish, stingy, self-centered
Gentle	Harsh, cruel, unkind, aggressive
Grateful	Ungrateful, thankless, unappreciative, entitled
Helpful	Unhelpful, hindering, unconstructive, critical
Honest	Dishonest, deceptive, deceitful, biased, manipulative
Hopeful	Hopeless, apathetic, depressed, unenthusiastic, despairing
Hospitable	Cold, unsociable, unfriendly, uninterested
Humble	Prideful, conceited, pretentious, arrogant
Initiative	Apathetic, dependent, inactive, lethargic
Integrity	Dishonest, dishonorable, corrupt, fake, manipulative
Joyful	Depressed, gloomy, miserable, sorrowful
Kind	Unkind, inconsiderate, discourteous, thoughtless
Loving	Unloving, aloof, indifferent, antagonistic
Optimistic	Pessimistic, hopeless, dejected, depressed
Other-centered	Self-centered, selfish, proud, isolated
Patient	Impatient, agitated, intolerant
Peaceful	Disturbed, agitated, argumentative, critical
Persevering	Fickle, unsteadfast, lazy
Polite	Impolite, rude, discourteous, inconsiderate
Remorseful	Unrepentant, callous, unashamed, prideful
Resilient	Fragile, weak, perfectionistic, fearful
Resourceful	Uncreative, stuck, helpless, apathetic, inactive, unimaginative

Healthy Quality	Some Opposite, Unhealthy Qualities
Respectful	Disrespectful, inconsiderate, discourteous, rude, condescending
Responsible	Irresponsible, unaccountable, independent
Self-control	Impulsive, unaware, inconsistent
Self-efficacy	Self-centered, not contributing, not purposeful, ineffective
Self-respect	Self-hatred, dishonor, self-doubt, self-neglect
Sincere	Insincere, deceitful, counterfeit
Submissive	Disobedient, resistant, disagreeable, prideful
Teachable	Prideful, hard-headed, resistant, easily satisfied
Unselfish	Selfish, greedy, uncharitable, arrogant

ACKNOWLEDGMENTS

I'm grateful God drew me to Himself so I was no longer satisfied being a church-attending good girl. My relationship with the God of the Bible as my Creator and Father; Jesus, His Son, as my Savior and Lord; and the Holy Spirit as my Teacher and Companion changed me. (That's an understatement!) I am who I am because of Him and I do what I do because of Him.

I can say the same thing about my parents and extended family. I'm grateful my brother, cousins, and I were expected to use good character and had many positive role models. I know the difference good character makes and I know it can be taught. I am who I am and I do what I do because of my parents and grandparents.

Without the support of many people, I couldn't have written this book. John Hannigan, our Executive Director, and his wife,

Melissa, an important thinker, example to me, author, and speaker, lead the list. Because John plans and manages so much of the ministry, I can concentrate on writing and teaching. I'm so glad God brought the three of us together! I also continue to be very grateful for my team at Moody Publishers, and Brian and Becky, my agents at Premiere Speakers Bureau. My Board of Directors also believes in me and helps to make ministry easy.

Linda, Dr. Gideon, Dr. Hanby, Dr. Snider, Shonda, and Jason keep me as healthy and as strong as possible and I am thankful. My schedule and the demands of travel are hard on my body!

I'm grateful for friends, thought leaders, prayer warriors, including those from my church. In particular, Steve and Joyce Baker challenged some of my ideas in the best way. When I was overwhelmed, their insights were a definite turning point. I also pray you have friends like Kayla, Linda, Julie, Dede, Lauren, and Andrea. They never minded discussing the ideas in these pages and they kept me sane.

NOTES

Chapter 1: What Is Character, and Why Does It Matter?

1. "Word History: The Characteristics of 'Character,'" Merriam-Webster, https://www.merriam-webster.com/words-at-play/word-history-of-character-origins.
2. Lee Nienhuis, *Countercultural Parenting: Building Character in a World of Compromise* (Eugene, OR: Harvest House Publishers, 2000), 27–28.
3. Os Guinness and Virginia Mooney, *When No One Sees: The Importance of Character in an Age of Image* (Colorado Springs: NavPress, 2020), 15–16.
4. Read Matthew, Mark, Luke, and John in the New Testament to learn about Jesus' life on earth.
5. As you read the Bible, look for consistency in the ways God interacts with different types of people, how and when His emotions are obvious, and what others say about Him. Also, studying His names will always help you understand His character.
6. 2 Timothy 2:15.
7. Matthew 28:18; John 1:12.
8. 1 John 1:9.
9. John 14:16–17.
10. 1 Thessalonians 2:4; 4:1; Matthew 22:36–38; 1 John 4:8; Isaiah 43:7; Psalm 86:12; 1 Corinthians 6:20; 1 Peter 4:16.
11. Matthew 6:9–13.
12. Jeremiah 17:9; Psalm 14:1–3; Mark 10:18; Romans 3:10–12; Ephesians 2:8–9.
13. I'm grateful to John Hannigan, our Executive Director, for helping me see the relevance of these three standards.
14. John 10:10.
15. Nienhuis, *Countercultural Parenting*, 39.

16. Isaiah 64:8; Psalm 139:13–14; Ephesians 2:10; and examples like Esther, Daniel, Moses, and Jeremiah.
17. Ephesians 2:10.

Chapter 2: How Do Children Develop Mature Character to Affect Culture?

1. Luke 2:52 NLT.
2. John 14:26; John 16:13–15; John 16:7–8; Acts 1:8; Romans 8:10–11; Romans 8:26–27; 1 Corinthians 3:16; 1 Corinthians 12:7–11; Galatians 5:16–25; Ephesians 1:13; and Ephesians 1:17–20.
3. Stephen Carter, *Integrity* (New York: Harper Perennial, 1996). Michael A. Zigarelli, *Cultivating Christian Character: How to Become the Person God Wants You to Be and How to Help Others Do the Same* (Colorado Springs: Purposeful Design, 2005).
4. Jonathan and Erica Catherman, *Raising Them Ready: Practical Ways to Prepare Your Kids for Life on Their Own* (Grand Rapids, MI: Revell, 2022), 55.
5. Kathy Koch, *Screens and Teens: Connecting with Our Kids in a Wireless World* (Chicago: Moody Publishers, 2015).
6. E. J. Dionne Jr., "Why the public interest matters now," *Daedalus, the Journal of the American Academy of Arts & Sciences* 136, no. 4 (Fall 2007): 8.
7. John Stonestreet and Brett Kunkle, *A Practical Guide to Culture: Helping the Next Generation Navigate Today's World* (Colorado Springs: David C. Cook, 2017), 27.
8. Ibid., 28.
9. Ibid., 36.
10. Ibid., 32.
11. Ibid., 31–32.
12. Koch, *Screens and Teens*, 172.
13. Matthew 6:9–13.

Chapter 3: How Are Character and Obedience Connected?

1. Os Guinness and Virginia Mooney, *When No One Sees: The Importance of Character in an Age of Image* (Colorado Springs: NavPress, 2000), 16.
2. See Stephen Carter, *Integrity* (New York: Harper Perennial, 1996), and Michael A. Zigarelli, *Cultivating Christian Character: How to Become the Person God Wants You to Be and How to Help Others Do the Same* (Colorado Springs: Purposeful Design, 2005).
3. This is especially true for the fruit of the Spirit. If joy and gratitude are present, it's more likely that children will also demonstrate other "fruit" qualities. "But the fruit of the Spirit is love, joy, peace, patience, kindness, goodness, faithfulness, gentleness, self-control; against such things there is no law" (Galatians 5:22–23). See Zigarelli, *Cultivating Christian Character.*
4. Zigarelli, *Cultivating Christian Character*, 23–24, 39–47.
5. Ibid., 42.
6. Ibid., 37.

Chapter 4: What Are Some Core Ways to Choose Qualities?

1. Kathy Koch, *Five to Thrive: How to Determine if Your Core Needs Are Being Met (and What to Do When They're Not)* (Chicago: Moody Publishers, 2020).
2. Kathy Koch, *8 Great Smarts: Discover and Nurture Your Child's Intelligences*, 28–33; *Resilient Kids: Raising Them to Embrace Life with Confidence*, 87–89; *Screens and Teens: Connecting with Our Kids in a Wireless World*, 15–30; *Start with the Heart: How to Motivate Your Kids to Be Compassionate, Responsible, and Brave (Even When You're Not Around)*, 89–109; Jill Savage and Kathy Koch, *No More Perfect Kids: Love Your Kids for Who They Are*, 91–94.
3. Lee Nienhuis, *Counter Cultural Parenting: Building Character in a World of Compromise* (Eugene, OR: Harvest House Publishers, 2020), 27–28.
4. *Five to Thrive* details how God meets these needs.
5. Koch, *8 Great Smarts*, 40.
6. Melissa Hannigan, *Inconvenient Parenting: Activate Your Child's God-Given Traits* (Chicago: Moody Publishers, 2023). You will love my colleague's book. Melissa will help you understand the benefits of playfulness and imagination, among other traits, that can make parenting challenging but life richer for children (and you)!
7. Email personal communication, March 19, 2023.
8. Koch, *Screens and Teens*.
9. We recommend Techless Wisephones because they come with only essential tools young people may need and they don't include games or access to the internet or social media: www.techless.com.

Chapter 5: What Biblical Truths Will Help You Choose Qualities?

1. John 17:17–19.
2. Many verses support these qualities. For example, 2 Thessalonians 3:3; James 5:11; Colossians 2:1–3; and Acts 13:38.
3. See Matthew 14:13–21 and Esther 4:5.
4. Jeffrey Kranz, "All the 'One Another' Commands in the NT [Infographic]," Overview Bible, March 9, 2014, https://overviewbible.com/one-another-infographic/. This post inspired me to think about categorizing the one-anothers.
5. "What Is a Worldview?," Summit Ministries, https://www.summit.org/worldview/.
6. Jeff Myers, *The Secret Battle of Ideas about God: Answers to Life's Biggest Questions* (Colorado Springs: David C. Cook, 2018).
7. Check out *The Picture-Smart Bible*, a Bible overview we sell, in a junior version and a regular version. You read a summary script for each book that includes the main events, people, and places. You and your children color in the outlined drawings so you have a visual summary of each book. It's a wonderful worldview product because children will see why God includes each book in the Bible. The big-picture overview will help them think about their lives: https://ckonlinestore.com/products/download-picture-smart-bible-starter-pack.

8. There are many chronological Bibles available. My church uses this one because it's very readable. *The One Year Chronological Bible (New Living Translation)* (Carol Stream, IL: Tyndale House Publishers, 2015).

9. Kathy Koch, *Start with the Heart: How to Motivate Your Kids to Be Compassionate, Responsible, and Brave (Even When You're Not Around)* (Chicago: Moody Publishers, 2019), 118–21.

Chapter 6: What Foundational Beliefs Are Essential?

1. 1 Samuel 2:2; Psalm 89:13–14; Isaiah 28:16.

2. Kathy Koch, *Screens and Teens: Connecting with Our Kids in a Wireless World* (Chicago: Moody Publishers, 2015), 175–178. See also Jean Wilund, "What Is the Authority of Scripture, and How Can We Trust It?," Bible Study Tools, August 5, 2022, https://www.biblestudytools.com/bible-study/topical-studies/what-is-the-authority-of-scripture-and-how-can-we-trust-it.html.

3. In addition to the verses I included in the chapter, you could read and reflect on these: Matthew 18:10; 21:15–16; Mark 5:37–43; 7:24–30; 9:33–37, 42; Luke 18:15–17; and John 4:46–54.

4. Park Row Christian Academy, Arlington, TX, July 13, 2007.

5. Kathy Koch, *Resilient Kids: Raising Them to Embrace Life with Confidence* (Chicago: Moody Publishers, 2022), 174–75. In this appendix, I list beliefs children must have about parents that are especially important if you want children to be resilient.

6. Genesis 2–3.

7. Informal "research" from April 4, 2023.

8. I've written about the change process in entire chapters in *Five to Thrive, Start with the Heart,* and *No More Perfect Kids* (written with Jill Savage).

9. I included some of these qualities in chapter 2 of *Start with the Heart.* I elaborate on some of these ideas there. Definitions are also paraphrased from dictionary.com and influenced by Michael Zigarelli's excellent book *Cultivating Christian Character.*

10. Michael A. Zigarelli, *Cultivating Christian Character: How to Become the Person God Wants You to Be and How to Help Others Do the Same* (Colorado Springs: Purposeful Design, 2005), 27.

11. Koch, *Resilient Kids.*

Chapter 7: What Strategies Can You Use for Teaching Character? (Part One)

1. I write about why I call these relational activities and not the typical Christian disciplines in the spiritual resiliency chapter in *Resilient Kids.* Other details about helping your children take them seriously may inspire you too.

2. My favorite resource for stories about missionaries and other Christian heroes, in book and audio form, is YWAM (ywampublishing.com). They have hundreds to choose from and are great for the family to read or listen to together.

3. 1 Corinthians 15:33.

4. Kathy Koch, *Five to Thrive: How to Determine if Your Core Needs Are Being Met (and What to Do When They're Not)* (Chicago: Moody Publishers, 2020). In the belonging

chapter, on pages 132–35, I share many details about four friendship skills: choosing friends wisely, conversation skills, maintaining relationships and resolving conflicts, and ending relationships when appropriate. On pages 136–138, I explain four friendship levels that can help children guard their hearts. All children benefit from these and they're especially important if your children are being led astray by peers.

5. Micah 7:19; Isaiah 38:17; Isaiah 43:25; Hebrews 8:12.
6. Daniel 1:8.
7. Esther 2:20.
8. Proverbs 18:21.
9. Kathy Koch, *Start with the Heart: How to Motivate Your Kids to Be Compassionate, Responsible, and Brave (Even When You're Not Around)* (Chicago: Moody Publishers, 2019). On pages 205–34, in chapter 9, I teach about complimenting and correcting well. I elaborate on these ideas and include many others that will help you encourage your children.
10. See Proverbs 15:32.
11. Koch, *Start with the Heart*. I fully share insights about natural and logical consequences on pages 149–56.

Chapter 8: What Strategies Can You Use for Teaching Character? (Part Two)

1. Kathy Koch, *Resilient Kids: Raising Them to Embrace Life with Confidence* (Chicago: Moody Publishers, 2022), 87–121.
2. Kathy Koch, *Five to Thrive: How to Determine if Your Core Needs Are Being Met (and What to Do When They're Not)* (Chicago: Moody Publishers, 2020), 177–81.
3. John 2:25; 10:14.
4. Luke 4:1–13; John 1:1.
5. John 17:4.
6. Matthew 16:5–12 is one example. Some people have asked why none of the disciples were at the tomb when Jesus came out. He had predicted His death and resurrection many times!
7. Kathy Koch, *8 Great Smarts: Discover and Nurture Your Child's Intelligences* (Chicago: Moody Publishers, 2016). See also Koch, *Start with the Heart: How to Motivate Your Kids to Be Compassionate, Responsible, and Brave (Even When You're Not Around)* (Chicago: Moody Publishers, 2019), 241–47 for concise definitions of each smart and a concise list of teaching suggestions for each.
8. Walter Barbe and Raymond H. Swassing, *Teaching Through Modality Strengths: Concepts and Practices* (Columbus: Zaner-Bloser, Inc., 1979). See also Koch, *Start with the Heart*, 237–39.
9. Tricia Goyer and Amy Parker, *The Grumbles: A Story about Gratitude* (New York: Running Press Kids, 2021).

ABOUT KATHY KOCH, PHD, CELEBRATE KIDS, INC., and IGNITE THE FAMILY

Dr. Kathy Koch (pronounced "cook") founded Celebrate Kids in 1991 to partner with parents to strengthen family relationships, develop children's unique gifts and talents, and equip them to live on purpose with intentionality. Because the chaotic culture has made parenting more difficult and the multigenerational family more important than ever, she became a founding associate of Ignite the Family with John and Melissa Hannigan in 2021. Just like Celebrate Kids, this is a faith-based ministry. Kathy will always celebrate kids, but it's time for a name change that reflects her heart and supports her, Melissa's, and John's current mission and passion. Through Ignite the Family, they will help the multigenerational family develop a biblical worldview and more.

Dr. Kathy has influenced thousands of parents, teachers, and children in thirty countries through keynote messages, seminars, chapels, fundraising banquets, and other events. She is proud to be represented by the Premiere Speakers Bureau and is a featured speaker for Teach Them Diligently and a regular presenter for Care Net, Summit Ministries, and the Colson Center. She speaks regularly at conferences, schools, churches, and pregnancy resource centers. The ministry also meets needs through an extensive product line, social media, and podcasts.

Dr. Kathy is also a popular guest on Focus on the Family radio and other radio talk shows and podcasts. She has been an expert in two of Kirk Cameron's documentary movies. This is her seventh book for Moody Publishers. The others are *Resilient Kids, Five to Thrive, Screens and Teens, 8 Great Smarts, Start with the Heart,* and *No More Perfect Kids* (with Jill Savage).

Dr. Kathy earned a PhD in reading and educational psychology from Purdue University. She was a tenured associate professor of education at the University of Wisconsin–Green Bay, a teacher of second graders, a middle school coach, and a school board member before becoming a full-time conference and keynote speaker in 1991. She has loved Jesus for years and her faith and desire to serve and glorify God is the foundation of her ministry.

WEBSITES:

www.CelebrateKids.com

www.IgniteTheFamily.com

FACEBOOK:

www.facebook.com/celebratekidsinc

www.facebook.com/ignitethefamily

INSTAGRAM:

www.instagram.com/celebratekidsinc

www.instagram.com/ignitethefamily

PODCASTS:

Celebrate Kids with Dr. Kathy, Facing the Dark, Dr. Kathy Says, and *Childlike Faith with Ella Hannigan*